LESSONS IN GRACE

LESSONS IN GRACE

TRUE STORIES ABOUT GOD WORKING IN AND THROUGH A
POLICE OFFICER

MATTHEW SPRINGER

WALK BY FAITH
MEDIA
WALKBYFAITHMEDIA.COM

I thank God for my loving wife, Daphney,
who stands back-to-back with me in my battles.

CONTENTS

·

Like most people, my earliest impressions of police work came primarily from TV shows and movies. From a young age, I knew the Hollywood version was not exceptionally accurate, but I had no idea just how far off that version could be at times.

Then I started volunteering as a police chaplain, and everything changed. I wasn't sure what to expect in the early days. But I knew God had called me into that line of ministry. It was a journey into a world that most people in non-first-responder jobs rarely, if ever, see. At times, soldiers and first responders see, smell, and hear things no human should ever have to experience.

It was in my capacity as a police chaplain that I first met Officer Matt Springer. I don't remember all the details of the day we met, but the officer I was riding with that shift had been asked to perform a welfare check on someone. Based on the information dispatch had relayed to the officer, there was reasonable cause to enter the house and one of the residents had granted permission. But as is often the case on such calls, there was no answer at the door. And, of course, the door was locked.

The officer requested assistance and asked if anyone on duty could pick a lock, so we could get in without having to wait for a locksmith or kick in the door. Lock picking was one of Matt's skills. Soon after he showed up, we were inside the house. I recall meeting Matt because it was the first time I'd seen an officer pick a lock.

As it turned out, the person to be checked on wasn't even home. The house was unoccupied. So, we relocked the door and left.

Aside from it being the first time seeing someone pick a lock on duty, nothing really stood out from that call, except that Matt was friendly and cordial. He had a reputation for always being available and willing to help . . . a hard worker. I saw Matt on a few other calls and had some casual conversations with him. But I didn't really get to know him until many months later.

I first rode with Matt about a year later. Nothing stood out from that first ride either, except that it was the start of a great friendship and the beginning of many adventures together. Over time though, one thing did stand out. There had been a dramatic change in Matt's life. He was not the person I'd met the night he picked that lock.

If you spend much time with Matt now, it's apparent that he is a man of solid faith, fully devoted to the kingdom of God. But in the early days of riding with him, he was fully devoted to catching bad guys and protecting the jurisdiction he was assigned to. He always had an eye out for trouble, listening for the next call. As with other officers, I watched with keen interest as he tracked down clues and interviewed both victims and suspects. He paid great attention to detail.

Between the time I first met him and the time I started riding with him, Matt had become a Christian. But he was not a mature one at first. He was not "seasoned" as we came to call it. This was still his Christian rookie year.

Then over time, that began to change. As his relationship with Jesus Christ began to mature, Matt changed, sometimes rapidly. He displayed more compassion. He began to exhibit a Godly love toward both the victims and the criminals.

There was still a time and a need for justice. Yet, he started to address the real, deeper, spiritual needs of the people he encountered, including those who were suspected of committing a crime. They needed to know that same *grace* he had found.

John the Baptist was once questioned by his followers about the growing number of people following Jesus. John replied, "He [Jesus] must increase, but I must decrease" (John 3:30 (NKJV)). That reminds me of what I was seeing in Matt's life. The better he got to know Jesus, the more his work and life centered on Jesus, instead of on himself and what he could achieve.

Because of the "low lives" Jesus associated with, he was accused of being a winebibber and a glutton (Matthew 11:19). His enemies looked down on him because he hung around with people like fishermen, poor people, prostitutes, and tax collectors. (Tax collectors were considered government-condoned thieves who robbed Jews to give money to Rome.) Jesus hung around with (and healed) lepers, lame men, and other undesirables.

Matt began sharing the power of God with victims who needed comfort in messed-up situations. He would pray on the way to a call and often prayed with the people he encountered there. When it was possible, he shared Biblical truth with the victims of crime. And he often shared the gospel with the suspects he arrested too.

As Matt's relationship with Jesus grew, he went from being a fully devoted cop to a fully devoted evangelist, even when some looked down on him for caring about the suspects (who some would call "low lives"). Matt found that the two could be done together. In fact, they were a perfect fit.

Being a police officer put him in situations where nobody else could go. Besides the normal "excitement" of police work, this gospel-police combo led to some wild adventures. I was honored to share in many of them.

By the time I started riding with Matt, I'd seen enough of the worst of people and situations in our city. In my experience, there were few surprises. But God put him (and, at times, us) in new situations where he could be used to minister to people. Hurting people. Bad people. People like Jesus had ministered to and called to be saved. Matt transformed from a man dedicated to protecting and saving the city to a man focused on helping individuals and letting them know that God could save *them*.

After several thousand hours of rides all over the city, I don't remember nearly all the details of the many situations I encountered with Matt. Often, memories come back when I pass by the site where an event occurred. But some memories are lost forever.

As this book brings some memories back, I'm reminded that they are beyond the common occurrences in typical police work. Instead, they are accounts of how *God* was working. God still moves in amazing ways. He is and has always been an awesome, amazing God. He changes lives, sometimes radically. His grace is amazing.

If you're interested in *real* police work (not the Hollywood version) *and* in how God moves in and through people's lives, read on. It will be well worth your time.

—Chaplain Dave Wurst

INTRODUCTION

Never in my wildest dreams did I think I would write a book. I had never really fancied myself a writer. And it had never been an interest of mine. Besides, rough and tough police officer types don't bother themselves with that kind of thing.

But since I was saved from my foolishness by God through His Son, Jesus Christ, I have seen all sorts of changes in my daily life. That rough and tough police officer exterior I thought I had seemed to just melt away. My heart had been hijacked by a Power I could have never predicted—I was in the grip of God's grace. I had no idea that my police career would take a miraculous turn or that, what I thought a police officer was supposed to be, would become more and more conformed into the image of the One who had saved me—Jesus Christ.

The Bible tells us that, when we are born again of the Spirit of God, we are cleansed of the sinful debt owed to God—the debt that kept us from having a true and lasting relationship with Him. It also teaches us that the Spirit of God gives us gifts. These are talents we gravitate to that allow us, His Church, to further the work of God while here on the earth.

I have always liked teaching. I love the rush I feel from standing in front of others and proclaiming something I'm really passionate about. It has been that way since high school. That gift never really came as a surprise. But I never thought in a million years that writing would become a main part of my worship back to Him.

Over the last few years, the Lord has given me a fervor for studying His word. He has shown me how the Bible isn't just a bunch of old, dusty stories from a time long past. The Scriptures are absolutely relevant even in the current day!

Then, I started to see how these truths began to show themselves in my day-to-day police work. I had to tell someone about it. So, I started writing them down.

As I read back through the years of stories I had compiled, I could see how God had been working in my life and the lives of those I served as an officer through something Christians call grace. Before we can go further, we need to define grace. It's imperative that we understand grace because the entire gospel of salvation through Jesus is predicated on the amazing fact that the Creator of the universe gives us grace.

The Bible speaks of three terms God has woven together throughout man's history: *justice*, *mercy*, and *grace*. As a police officer, I have worked closely with justice and mercy.

Justice is simple; it is getting what you deserve. If you rob a bank at gunpoint and are caught by the police, you'll be arrested and thrown in jail. Through the court process, you'll be found guilty (by evidence) of breaking the law that makes it illegal to take something of value from another person by using a deadly weapon. You will also be given the prescribed punishment for the infraction detailed by the law. That punishment includes paying back restitution to the bank or the individual teller you terrorized in your crime spree. Thus, you and the victim both get what you deserve. You get punished, and the victim gets justice.

On the other hand, mercy is when you *don't* get what you deserve. If you were driving your new sports car at fifteen miles an hour over the speed limit and I pulled you over, you would deserve a speeding ticket. If I didn't give you a ticket but just a warning, that's mercy. Although you were verbally reprimanded for breaking the stated law of speed, you did not receive what you deserved—the dreaded traffic ticket.

But grace is something entirely different . . .

If we keep it simple like we did with the other two definitions, grace is defined as getting what you don't deserve. But this term is a bit harder to illustrate.

Let's suppose that you committed a financial crime by defrauding a handful of people out of their entire life savings. After a stellar police investigation, you were arrested and found guilty of your crime in court. The judge handed down, as punishment, a very steep fine that would help compensate the people you defrauded. The fine is so large that you have no hope of paying it in a timely manner, and you are facing a life sentence in jail as the alternative.

You have received what you deserve for your criminal actions, and the victims get a chance to be made whole again by receiving restitution. This is how our Judeo-Christian criminal justice system works. That is justice.

But what if a complete stranger walked into the courtroom and paid your fine with the cash in their retirement account so you could be let off the hook? That is grace.

You are getting an outcome you didn't earn and don't deserve, instead of the punishment that you actually deserve. And in this case, the punishment is being incurred by an innocent person. Justice says that a debt is always paid, either by the offender or by someone in the offender's place. But I've never seen someone pay a debt for an offender in the courtroom. There aren't many folks out there who see redeeming qualities in people convicted of egregious criminal behavior.

However, that's exactly what Jesus did for mankind. And if we look at grace from a Biblical point of view, it is better relayed as something God gives you, something you cannot earn on your own. Grace is a gift from God. When you are born again, God gives you liberty from the unpayable debt you incurred by living a sinful life.

Just as in the example above, Jesus Christ, who lived a sinless life, chose to die in your place to pay off your sinful debt that you have no way of paying. No amount of your own "good deeds" can pay the debt you have incurred over your lifetime. So, in doing this one loving and sacrificial act, Jesus has released you from the most daunting of eternal penalties . . . spiritual death and separation from God in hell.

This is the crux of the entire gospel narrative. And your comprehension of grace is the key to understanding God's love for you. As the Bible says:

> When we were utterly helpless, Christ came at just the right time and died for us sinners. Now, most people would not be willing to die for an upright person, though someone might perhaps be willing to die for a person who is especially good. But God showed His great love for us by sending Christ to die for us while we were still sinners. And

since we have been made right in God's sight by the blood of Christ, He will certainly save us from God's condemnation. For since our friendship with God was restored by the death of His Son while we were still His enemies, we will certainly be saved through the life of His Son. So now we can rejoice in our wonderful new relationship with God because our Lord Jesus Christ has made us friends of God. (Romans 5:6–11 (NLT))

The primary way the word *grace* is used in the Bible is interesting. The word refers to a gift, given to you by God—a gift you couldn't earn and didn't deserve. In essence, the gift is His purchase of your eternal salvation. But I want to show you that God's grace can be seen in all sorts of ways. And if you train yourself to see it, you will see it *everywhere*.

Throughout the pages of this book, I want you to ride along with me. Join me as I take you through some police calls that revealed the most amazing miracles I have ever been blessed and honored to witness. They might not be the most glamorous calls in the police world. But I think you will see why they've had such an impact on me and my Christian walk of faith.

It's my desire for you to see God's grace all around you. I want to show you how God uses His grace to develop a deeper love for Him in us and a more compassionate love for other people, even when those people are the ones you might not dare to love.

1 / THE CALLING

GOD'S GRACE GIVES US PURPOSE AND DIRECTION

LIKE MANY, September 11, 2001, was a pivotal day for me. I rolled out of bed after one of those "been traveling too long and I'm not in my own bed" kinds of sleepless nights. A few hours before, I had landed in Hawaii for a much-needed vacation. But when I saw what had happened on the mainland, I didn't have much of a heart for vacationing. I knew that things would never be the same. I spent most of that day watching the thick, black smoke rolling from the World Trade Center on the news.

Now, I can hear what you're thinking, *Tough place to be "locked down" after all the air traffic was halted for two or three days after the attacks.* But all I wanted was to be home where I was close to my loved ones. For all intents and purposes, our nation was under attack. We were at war.

Although I was a banker at the time, I had always dreamed of being a Navy SEAL—the best of the best. Yet, I had already graduated from college and had a number of good things happening in my life. I didn't want to be burdened with being deployed to the Middle East. Well actually, that's only what I told people. The truth was a little less glamorous: I didn't have the mental toughness to be a SEAL, and I was scared to death of the pending war.

Still, my heart was jolted into a place where I felt it was necessary to do *something* to protect my nation. I knew the local police SWAT team used the same weapons and tactics that the SEALs do. They were the "best of the best," and they were close to home. It made sense to fight the battle in my community. So, the next thing I knew, I had applied to become a police officer. I had a rough sketch of what my future plans looked like, but I had no idea what I was getting into.

Being a police officer was the greatest thing I had ever dared to do. And as each year went by, I learned more and more about people—the good *and* the bad. I discovered the dark veil that drapes all around us, just below the surface.

I realized it was a lot easier to live in complete oblivion to what was going on in the community, not because people weren't privy to finding it, but because they didn't really want to know. They didn't want to accept the truth that evil lurks everywhere . . . just under the surface. It's far easier to pretend it doesn't exist. That is until that evil comes calling. I decided I would be the one to defend the helpless from that evil, to be the sheepdog that protects the flock from the wolves.

It seems like people always ask the same questions. Questions like, "What was the scariest thing you've ever seen?" And, "What was the craziest thing you've ever had to do?"

For most police officers, their answers are the stories that they hang their badge and their egos on. Those are the stories the department rewards and the calls that lead to an officer's legacy and reputation.

I think back to the time I waded into an angry crowd at a skating rink to arrest a teenage girl who had hit another officer over the head with a roller skate. The crowd had closed in around us, and we were able to use pepper spray as a distraction to cover our escape through a side door before it got really violent.

Then there was the forty-car pileup on a major highway one April night when a bridge had iced over. I had to jump over a concrete highway barrier to avoid getting hit by a sliding car.

I remember the utter horror of confronting a mentally ill man who had tied off his arm with a t-shirt before cutting off his own hand because his inner monologue "told him" that his hand was his "enemy." I'm grateful for the supervisor who argued with the medics to protect the mental health of the officers who were involved.

I can still feel the anxiety of performing CPR on people who had collapsed in their family homes . . . while their loved ones looked on. And the feeling of heartache when neither myself nor the medical crews could bring them back from death.

I recall the sadness of talking to a young man who was the passenger in a car accident . . . and not telling him that the driver, his best friend, had been killed in the same accident. The sight of his friend's blood all over his jeans lingers in my mind.

Or that time when my only option was to ram my patrol car into the side of a wayward vehicle to stop it from causing more mayhem and property damage. We initially thought she was drunk, and we had to stop her so someone wouldn't be hurt or killed. As it turned out, she was having a medical emergency, so we probably saved her life too.

I can still see the aftermath of the high-speed pursuit with an armed man when his car crashed through a wooden fence. The police car behind him took a wooden fence plank right through the windshield. The plank narrowly missed the officer's head as his patrol car came to a stop. The Lord was certainly with him that night.

I have probably forgotten more stories than I can remember. But these aren't the calls that made lasting impacts on my life. As I sit here, contemplating the eighteen years I spent wearing a badge and enforcing the law, I recollect things that no man or woman should ever have to see. I think back to times when humanity showed absolute evil.

Yet, there were also times when people illuminated the darkness to expose the evil—when people pulled together, despite themselves, to offer love and grace to those in need. I look back on a time when my perception of what I thought police work was supposed to be had changed. And I recall the time when *everything* changed.

But before we can get to that, it needs some introduction.

I can relate to Paul the Apostle in many ways. Yet, none of his adventures, sufferings, wins, and losses are more relatable to me than the time he was confronted by Jesus on the road to Damascus.

Paul, who was known as Saul at the time, was zealous to enforce God's law. As a member of the religious Sanhedrin, Saul had been educated by the best and brightest scholars and teachers in Israel. He knew the law like the back of his hand, and he was driven to enforce that law against those who broke it. That included the followers of Jesus. In fact, the Bible tells us that Paul thought this emphatic work was for God's benefit (*see* Acts 22:3–5; 1 Corinthians 15:9–10).

For the first twelve years of my police career, I was enthusiastic about enforcing the law, just like Saul. However, this law was the law of our city, county, and state. I had compassion for those who were victims. But if you victimized people, I was coming after you.

I didn't care who you were or why you did it. Whether you were a drunk driver, a drug addict, a homeless man who took food, or a single mother with kids who couldn't afford diapers, if you broke the law, you went to jail. I was zealous to do what my department had trained me to do. I was driven to uphold my oath of office. And I was striving to get accepted into the elite special assignment—the best of the best—the SWAT team.

Yet, just like Saul, things were about to change: both in my career and my heart. Up to that point, the SWAT team had eluded me. And I started to wonder what I was missing. But it wasn't *what* I was missing as much as *whom* I was missing. And Saul was about to find out this truth too.

As it tells us in the Book of Acts:

> Then Saul, still breathing threats and murder against the disciples of the Lord, went to the high priest and asked letters from him to the synagogues of Damascus, so that if he found any who were of the Way, whether men or women, he might bring them bound to Jerusalem.
>
> As he journeyed he came near Damascus, and suddenly a light shone around him from heaven. Then he fell to the

ground, and heard a voice saying to him, "Saul, Saul, why
are you persecuting Me?"

And he said, "Who are You, Lord?"

Then the Lord said, "I am Jesus, whom you are persecuting.
It is hard for you to kick against the goads."

So he, trembling and astonished, said, "Lord, what do You
want me to do?" (Acts 9:1–6 (NKJV))

Once proud and arrogant, Saul was now lying on the ground,
afraid of what had just happened. He was in the grip of Jesus
Christ, and his life was changing in a dramatic fashion. I can't
say my transformation in that same loving grip of Jesus was this
dramatic, but I can tell you it was intense enough for me.

I had been in the throes of a life-altering addiction for around
twenty years. Although I had tried everything known to secular
mankind, I had not been able to shake it. It destroyed my first
marriage and my self-esteem. Looking back, I can see the trail
of destruction I left throughout decades of relationships. I had
nowhere else to turn.

But a strong, Christian woman, who is now my wife, saw a
different picture. And when she introduced me to Jesus, I had
finally come to the end of myself. The addiction had cost me a
lot of time. I had a lot of regrets, and I didn't want to lose her
too. So, I took her advice and prayed earnestly through a book
on spiritual warfare that she had given me. I didn't really
believe in that stuff, but I felt I needed to pray through it
anyway.

Saul found himself overwhelmed by Jesus and blinded by the
light that had come from His presence. He was led by the hand
into Damascus, blind and humbled. He sat there, not eating or

drinking anything. After three days, Ananias, an obedient disciple of Jesus, courageously prayed over and baptized the feared man known as Saul. This led to his miraculous transformation into a man named Paul, zealous to teach and preach the gospel of Jesus Christ. He would be known for taking the gospel message all over the known world.

The Bible tells us:

> And Ananias went his way and entered the house; and laying his hands on him he said, "Brother Saul, the Lord Jesus, who appeared to you on the road as you came, has sent me that you may receive your sight and be filled with the Holy Spirit." Immediately there fell from his eyes something like scales, and he received his sight at once; and he arose and was baptized.
>
> So when he had received food, he was strengthened. Then Saul spent some days with the disciples at Damascus. (Acts 9:17–19 (NKJV))

It can be hard for a skeptic to believe in that kind of radical personality change. I would have been skeptical myself if it hadn't happened to me.

After I surrendered to Jesus, the extreme draw of my addiction mysteriously vanished. And it has never returned. I can't tell you why. I only know that my prayer was answered.

It was clear that I needed this kind of power in my life because, up until that point, I had messed up everything I had ever done. The control I thought I had was just an illusion, and now the scales had fallen from my eyes. I could see clearly. I could see that, without God, I was nothing.

A few months later, I was baptized for the second time. (Although it was really the first time because, if you're not a believer, like I wasn't as a teenager, the only thing that happens when you get baptized is you just get wet.) I felt different when I came up out of that reservoir water, but I kept it to myself. It was time to go on shift.

Paul's change was so dynamic that he went from wanting to arrest and kill those who believed in Jesus, to spending time with Christians and even teaching Jesus in the synagogues. The Bible tells us:

> Immediately he preached the Christ in the synagogues, that He is the Son of God.
>
> Then all who heard were amazed, and said, "Is this not he who destroyed those who called on this name in Jerusalem, and has come here for that purpose, so that he might bring them bound to the chief priests?"
>
> But Saul increased all the more in strength, and confounded the Jews who dwelt in Damascus, proving that this Jesus is the Christ. (Acts 9:20–22 (NKJV))

I had no idea that all of this would completely change the way I would conduct myself as a police officer and that my view of people (who are made in the image of God) would change from that day on. Looking back, I can see that I went from being a man like Saul, zealous to enforce the law and put bad guys in jail, to a man like Paul, who loved and cherished people —a man zealous to show the love and grace of Jesus Christ to those who are lost.

As it turned out, my career and my legacy weren't made by those crazy and scary calls I mentioned earlier. My heart wasn't strengthened by my dreams of being a SWAT officer. My soul and spirit were not purified by the pursuit of departmental accolades. All those things were instilled in my soul when I realized that I was working for an audience of One . . . God.

So, what follows are stories of God's grace—the grace He showed to me and to those I met on police calls. The stories are about the times God showed up, not in the "wind" or the "earthquake" or the "fire"—not in the crazy and the scary—but in a "still small voice" (1 Kings 19:11–12 (NKJV)). These are the stories that influenced my walk with Christ the most. They penetrated my soul and gave me evidence that God is real and walks among us. And they show how much God truly loves His creation and how nothing occurs by happenstance.

I want to share these stories with you. This book has been five years in the making . . . although I had no idea when I started writing that it would go this far.

Our walk with the Lord needs time, patience, and maturity. I'm reminded of what the Lord told the prophet Jeremiah when he went into the potter's house.

> The word which came to Jeremiah from the LORD, saying: "Arise and go down to the potter's house, and there I will cause you to hear My words." Then I went down to the potter's house, and there he was, making something at the wheel. And the vessel that he made of clay was marred in the hand of the potter; so he made it again into another vessel, as it seemed good to the potter to make.
>
> Then the word of the LORD came to me, saying: "O house of Israel, can I not do with you as this potter?" says the LORD. "Look, as the clay is in the potter's hand, so are you in My hand, O house of Israel!" (Jeremiah 18:1–6 (NKJV))

I can look back and see where God has broken me down to rebuild me. I can see times when I have been shaped and molded into something new, something different. It has been hard but rewarding. And I don't think He is done.

Things are changing yet again, so I cannot say that I have attained perfection. Instead, I am continually refined in the fires of life into what He wants me to be as I move into the next season of my life. I hope the stories in this book will encourage you.

God's grace is so evident in my life. Looking back on the things I have done, I don't deserve the unmerited favor God has shown me through the years. But I make it a point not to argue with the Creator of the universe, who has shown me how powerful He truly is. Paul didn't think he deserved it either when he said:

> This is a trustworthy saying, and everyone should accept it: "Christ Jesus came into the world to save sinners"—and I am the worst of them all. But God had mercy on me so that Christ Jesus could use me as a prime example of his great patience with even the worst sinners. Then others will realize that they, too, can believe in him and receive eternal life. (1 Timothy 1:15–16 (NLT))

If Paul, who had killed Christians, can be saved by the hands of God's grace, and if I can be saved and used powerfully by God's grace, then you can be too. I promise.

I hope these stories strengthen your faith. And I hope you are moved to walk a little closer to the Lord. Because He is there, calling. Once you see the hand of God in everyday things, you will see His hand in everything you do.

2 / THE GUY IN THE CAR

GOD'S GRACE IS WILDLY UNPREDICTABLE

WORKING as a police officer has a lot of "downtime." I've heard it said that police work is 99 percent boredom followed by 1 percent of sheer terror. I suppose that's a fair assessment. And for the most part, the slow times are just a chance to collect your thoughts.

But what do you do when you're taken off-guard while you're simply sitting in your car doing paperwork? I was in my police car writing reports and waiting for my next dose of reality when I was approached by a flashy-looking car. I can remember it clearly—a jet-black Volkswagen with way too much chrome for a little car like that.

I had my car strategically positioned in a school's parking lot, where I would be able to see any car that entered my space. I had learned to be careful about those kinds of things. It was a protective measure so I wouldn't be caught off guard.

However, it was daytime. And I had become accustomed to people pulling up next to me, especially in that neighborhood, to ask for directions or thank me for my service. Still, it only takes danger to come knocking once to change everything. It was prudent to expect the unexpected. Yet, I had no idea that what was about to happen would set off a chain of events that would change my life forever.

After twelve years of seeing the dark side of life, I was shallow and hard-hearted. I had not realized any of my hopes and dreams—the ones that had led me to decide on police work in the first place. And I was struggling with my work identity.

But my life had been changing in other ways. It hadn't been very long since I had given my life to Christ and had been baptized. I had dawdled in rampant sin for a long time, and it had destroyed a lot of my life up to that point. But now the winds of change were upon me. I remember coming up out of the water and feeling like a different person.

God had done some amazing work in just a few short months. I was on a different path, one I hadn't expected. Thinking back, it reminded me of Jesus' words to a religious leader when He said:

> The wind blows where it wishes, and you hear the sound of it, but cannot tell where it comes from and where it goes. So is everyone who is born of the Spirit. (John 3:8 (NKJV))

I had no idea where this new feeling came from or how it was going to shape the direction of my life. Much like the wind, I could feel the effects of the Holy Spirit as He influenced me. But I couldn't explain it.

The driver of the little, black car was older, with snow-white hair and a loud Hawaiian shirt. I chuckled when I saw him. He reminded me of a used car salesman. I wasn't sure what he wanted to talk about, but I didn't feel particularly threatened. So I took my hand off my sidearm as I gave him a friendly hello.

The man told me that he was appreciative of my being around the neighborhood. He and his wife lived only a few blocks from the school where we were talking, and he was encouraged that I had taken a stance of being visible and available. None of this was crazy, I had heard this a lot. But it was the next thing he said . . .

You know? You aren't going to be a police officer forever. I see you doing something else. Maybe in a leadership position. Maybe a pastor of a church.

I felt my face tingle. Did I hear him right? Did he say "pastor?" My jaw proverbially hit the floor. I wasn't expecting that. How did he know that was a thought I had been having? How did he know my heart was steamrolling toward a desire for the ministry?

It took me a second to stabilize my thoughts. But before I could ask him for clarification, he said, "Well, see ya later." And he drove away.

What do I say to that? I sat in my patrol car, motionless and astonished. I couldn't explain what had just happened. I had no idea who he was. I had no idea where he lived. Even if I wanted clarification, I was never going to get it.

How on earth, of all the police officers in this city, did this slick-looking guy pull up next to the only officer I knew who had even an inkling in his mind about being a pastor? I had seen God do some pretty awesome stuff. Up until this moment, it was easy to explain each of them away in natural terms if my mindset wasn't right. But this?

Can I call this prophetic? Am I allowed to say this is a *calling*? My mind scrolled through the numerous stories in the Bible where God had done something jaw-dropping to call someone to a task. I thought about Moses. Listen to how the Bible tells us that Moses was called:

> And the Angel of the LORD appeared to him [Moses] in a flame of fire from the midst of a bush. So he looked, and behold, the bush was burning with fire, but the bush was not consumed. Then Moses said, "I will now turn aside and see this great sight, why the bush does not burn."
>
> So when the LORD saw that he turned aside to look, God called to him from the midst of the bush and said, "Moses, Moses!" (Exodus 3:2–4 (NKJV))

God would go on to tell Moses that He had commissioned him to lead the Israelites out of Egypt.

I also thought about the Prophet Samuel. The Bible tells us:

> Now the LORD had told Samuel in his ear the day before Saul came, saying, "Tomorrow about this time I will send you a man from the land of Benjamin, and you shall anoint him commander over My people Israel, that he may save My people from the hand of the Philistines; for I have looked upon My people, because their cry has come to Me."
>
> So when Samuel saw Saul, the LORD said to him, "There he is, the man of whom I spoke to you. This one shall reign over My people." (1 Samuel 9:15–17 (NKJV))

God had told Samuel to keep an eye out for a man from the land of Benjamin. At the same time, God supernaturally led Saul to the city where Samuel lived while looking for several missing donkeys that had wandered from his father's farm. Saul had no idea that, by the end of the day, he would be anointed by Samuel to be the king of Israel.

Or how about the prophet Jeremiah:

> Then the word of the LORD came to me [Jeremiah], saying: "Before I formed you in the womb I knew you; before you were born I sanctified you; I ordained you a prophet to the nations."
>
> Then said I: "Ah, Lord GOD! Behold, I cannot speak, for I am a youth."
>
> But the LORD said to me: "Do not say, 'I am a youth,' for you shall go to all to whom I send you, and whatever I command you, you shall speak. Do not be afraid of their faces, for I am with you to deliver you," says the LORD.
>
> Then the LORD put forth His hand and touched my mouth, and the LORD said to me:
>
> "Behold, I have put My words in your mouth." (Jeremiah 1:4–9 (NKJV))

There are stories like these all throughout the Bible. So many of them have supernatural aspects to them . . . things that couldn't be explained without the very hand of God. I couldn't explain what had happened to me either. God is so good. He actually made the circumstances "jaw-dropping" so I couldn't explain them away. It literally forced my hand and made me believe that God was in the details and had spoken to me.

Clearly, God has a specific calling for those who are born again of the Spirit. And He desires nothing short of complete obedience to His calling. If God went to this length to call me? *Wow.*

From that day forward, I started to look at police work as a ministry.

Not long after this, I was called to a house on the report of a stolen van. The victim was a lovely lady in her late eighties named Carol, and the suspect was her nephew, Scott. Carol had allowed Scott to stay at her house to get him away from bad influences that had led to serious drug and alcohol abuse. He had "borrowed" the van to run some errands. But over the next three days, she had not heard from him. So, she felt the need to call it in as stolen.

I had taken dozens of stolen car reports. Yet, this one was different. I don't know if it was because I had a different heart or because Carol was a tremendously powerful Christian woman, but the conversations and the subsequent relationship that developed were a breath of fresh air.

Carol had been a gospel singer whose beautiful voice had been taken from her by throat cancer. Her life had been full of trials, but she had remained faithful to the Lord through it all. Her bookshelf was lined with dozens of journals filled with prayers and songs she had written over the nearly seven decades that she had been walking with the Lord. Carol appeared to be the living illustration of what the Psalmist wrote in the Bible:

> The LORD is near to those who have a broken heart, and saves such as have a contrite spirit.
>
> Many are the afflictions of the righteous, but the LORD delivers him out of them all. (Psalm 34:18–19 (NKJV))

She was a powerful woman in Christ. And even after being wronged, I was amazed by her love for her nephew. Her heart was torn: she wasn't sure she wanted to make this report, but after her car had been taken from her for three days, she needed to get it back. It was her only mode of transportation. And at eighty-seven years old, she was still very active at church. We filed a stolen car report, and I left her home.

The next day, I heard that Scott had brought the van back. I jumped on the call, knowing that I would have a chance to work the stolen vehicle case to its logical conclusion. Now, I have to be cautious here when I say "logical" because I knew that the Lord would be in the details. I didn't know what to expect, and I wanted to be the one to see how the Lord was going to work it all out.

Carol was so gracious. As we sat in the living room, she told me that she wanted to forgive Scott and drop the charges. Her nephew knew he had been caught and was at the mercy of what she wanted to do. I saw him exhale when she let him off the hook.

If I were any other officer, I might have been a bit upset by her reversal. I had done all the work the night before to write the reports. And now, having the suspect in front of me—right where I wanted him? That's a good day for a police officer.

Yet, I know the Scriptures. And I know the God behind the Scriptures—how He desires us to forgive and restore those who have wronged us in a sense of love. Because of this, I was good to leave the story finished. But I told Carol and Scott that I was going to go through the van and make sure I didn't find any illegal contraband. Knowing his drug history and the story he told me about the drug bender he had been on, I was sure I would find something.

The van was filthy. Apparently, Scott had been living in the car, and he had not taken the time to clean up after himself. This tends to be a normal thing for drug addicts since they are only concerned about themselves. I was shocked that I only found one thing of interest in his disaster. And interestingly, the object was not illegal.

It was a Bible.

I took the book back into the house, and I threw it down on the glass coffee table in front of Scott. I asked him about it. He told me not to mess with his Bible. He told me that a guy on the street had given it to him, and it meant a lot to him.

I told him that it was the only thing in the van that had any value. I explained the love of Christ and how his aunt had lived by what was written in that book when she allowed him to escape arrest. And I told him how the same book had changed my heart and the way I did my job. It was the reason he wasn't already in handcuffs for his crimes.

I left Scott sitting with Carol. I went out to my patrol car to get the stolen van out of the national system and make sure that he didn't have warrants for other issues that might be hanging over his head. When I learned that he was clear, I walked back down the short cul-de-sac toward the house.

Scott met me on the sidewalk where he asked me an interesting question. "Are you an angel?"

Now, I will admit, I have been called many things in my career, but "angel" was not one of them. I chuckled slightly at the absurdity of the question. Then I told him, "No, I'm just a man who loves Jesus." He shook my hand, gave me a hug, and thanked me.

Over the next year, I would stop by and check in on Carol. We would talk and pray for each other, and she would tell me stories about her life. I got to know her son and daughter, and she always kept me apprised of what Scott was doing.

Amazingly, not long after our encounter, he stopped using drugs. He got involved in a Christian youth camp, serving and warning kids about the dangers of drugs, and sharing about the grace of our Lord. It was quite a resurrection story.

And just to bring this whole thing full circle . . .

One day, I was walking out of Carol's house after a wonderful conversation. I noticed a jet-black Volkswagen with too much chrome for a little car like that, parked neatly in the driveway next door. I was dumbfounded. Could it be?

I remember him saying he and his wife lived in the neighborhood. Yep, we were only a few blocks from the school where we had met the year before. I had been hoping I would find this guy one day. I wanted so badly to know why he had gone out of his way to tell me those words that had changed my life so drastically. I got up the courage, and I walked up to the door.

An older man with snow-white hair answered my knock. I would like to tell you that I immediately recognized him. But time had passed, and the thousands of people I had seen since that day had made my memory murky.

I told him that I was sorry to bother him and had an interesting question for him. I asked him if he happened to remember pulling up next to a police officer in his car in a parking lot and telling him that he would be a pastor one day. He said he did! I told him that it was me that he had spoken to and that my heart, since that day, had been burning with a desire to know why he had randomly done that.

His answer was simple. "The Lord told me to." I then learned that the man was a pastor from a local church and he aimed to be obedient to what the Lord wanted him to do. He said it was not a strange thing for him. And on that day, he had spoken from his heart.

I was amazed.

While I was telling him how his words had single-handedly changed the way I looked at police work, how I had come to know Christ, and how I had been thinking about ministry, the man's wife came outside to see what we were doing. I'm sure a police officer in your driveway, talking to your husband, would drum up some nervous curiosity.

He told her what we were talking about, and she too remembered the story. While she was speaking, she stopped as if she had seen something. She told me that she could see I was surrounded by angels, and they were there to protect me. She said that they would not allow any harm to come to me. I'm sure my jaw hit the floor again at this statement. Then, they both laid their hands on me and prayed for me before I left.

Boy, do I have a lot to learn.

Could she actually see angels around me? I don't really know. But I believe in angels. I believe they are there to protect us. And after a long career so far, I had been protected from all kinds of horrible things. So . . . I suppose you can be the judge of that.

But the supernatural calling that day and this unbelievable story fundamentally changed the way I saw people—both those deemed "good" and those deemed "bad." When you serve God and know that He redeemed you from your sinful life and called you to His service, you realize there is nothing that He won't do to save those who are made in His image.

And just like me, God is looking for you. The Bible tells us plainly:

> For the eyes of the LORD run to and fro throughout the whole earth, to show Himself strong on behalf of those whose heart is loyal to Him. (2 Chronicles 16:9 (NKJV))

God wants you to be obedient to a life He has engineered for you. If you keep your eyes open, the supernatural calling might come your way too. And I promise you, it will be worth it.

3 / A SECOND CHANCE

GOD'S GRACE GIVES US A DO-OVER

POLICE WORK certainly has its share of "frequent flyers," those people you see a lot because they just can't quite get it together. In the past, I really struggled to show compassion to those types of people. My rationale was simple: if you can't get it figured out the first time, I don't really have time for you anymore.

But that mentality is incredibly flawed. After I was saved by Jesus, my heart changed. The people I have to deal with more than once tend to give me a deeper understanding of how God probably saw me in my brokenness. After numerous times of going back and forth between Him and the world, He still pursued me. And once I figured it out—man, what a glorious transformation that was! I now see those I deal with on multiple occasions in a very different way. I see them through the eyes of a patient and loving God.

One such man, Chris, I hadn't seen for more than a year. The first time I dealt with Chris, he was high on meth and heavily intoxicated. I knew it was a very dangerous situation, and I prayed that God would deliver him safely into our custody without violence.

As the story unfolded, his father (a former police officer himself) told us that he had never seen Chris act like this before. He warned us that, if we went into the basement, Chris might use the revolver he had in his hands against us or himself. That didn't leave us with many options.

I found myself stationed on the back porch of the neighbor's house. Not very glamorous. But it gave me a bird's eye view of the backyard and time to pray.

When Chris, who was heavily intoxicated, walked out of the basement slider and into the backyard, I knew the incident was quickly deteriorating. If he got into the greenbelt with that gun, we were going to be in a very dangerous situation. All it would have taken was for him to walk across the backyard and through the gate.

But a funny thing happened that turned the tide. Instead of using the gate in the backyard, this man, in an alcoholic stupor, attempted to climb the fence into the neighbor's backyard. As you can predict, Chris fell off the fence and landed on his back. Then he got up and used the gate, leading the police on a treacherous chase into the greenbelt that runs behind the house.

When Chris saw the police following him, he went for the gun he had stashed in his waistband. But it wasn't there. The Lord had providentially used the fall from the fence to knock the gun out of his shorts and under the dried leaves that had collected in the corner of the backyard. Without his gun, he was taken into custody and placed into the back of an ambulance to get help.

I thanked the Lord for saving Chris's life. Although I didn't know it at the time, it was actually the second time God had saved his life that day.

Later, I opened up that revolver to check the rounds inside, I was shocked by what I found. There were only two bullets, and one had the primer pricked. That means Chris had pulled the trigger and the hammer had fallen on the round, but the bullet hadn't gone off. I found out later that Chris had pulled the trigger in front of his dad in an attempt to kill himself. God had saved his life by stopping his suicide too.

I was blown away that God had answered my prayer to deliver him to us without violence. I praised God's goodness to anyone on-scene who would listen. God is so good!

Almost six months later, I was able to tell Chris how God had saved his life that day. In teary-eyed desperation, he told me he wanted to change his life. I was able to lay my hands on him and pray for him. Soon after, he checked himself into rehab. But sadly, that didn't last long.

I found out a few months later that Chris's life was saved a third time when rescue personnel found him unresponsive in his car after he had overdosed on illicit narcotics. He was revived and taken to a hospital. Once again, he was spared due to the wonderful work of the medical personnel who revived him . . . and God's sovereign hands. God always has a plan.

And then I didn't hear his name again until nearly a year later.

In a drug-fueled rage and under tremendous paranoia, he again tried to take his own life with pills. It took six cops to get him under control so he could be placed in an ambulance. I couldn't get there in time to see him. I walked up to the house as the ambulance pulled away.

I had always wondered if he had died an untimely death or was in jail. I was shocked that he was still alive. I was also surprised that, instead of being indignant toward him, I found my heart burning to talk to him.

His dad told me that he had been doing very well. He had taken care of his jail time (a blessing from the Lord) and had gotten himself a good job. He had been staying away from drugs and alcohol and had been reading the Bible every day. Unfortunately, this had all changed over the past week, and Chris was now back in the grip of illegal drugs and all that could come with them.

I was surprised at how much I found myself caring for him. This guy had fought with police officers, terrorized his own family, been tazed, and a plethora of other things that don't get you well-liked among police officers. But to my amazement, I didn't see him in that way. Why had God saved his life so many times? And why did my heart care so much about him?

I was reminded of this passage in the Bible:

> But, beloved, do not forget this one thing, that with the Lord one day is as a thousand years, and a thousand years as one day. The Lord is not slack concerning His promise, as some count slackness, but is longsuffering toward us, not willing that any should perish but that all should come to repentance. (2 Peter 3:8–9 (NKJV))

Peter tells us that time is not a factor in God's economy. His *year* and His *day* are the same length of time. But Peter says that God is patient with us. He doesn't want anyone to be destroyed by their failure to come to Him for salvation. God gives ample time to fix the issue.

And it certainly appeared that this was how this young man's story was unfolding. God had been tremendously patient with Chris.

And thinking back to my stubbornness—if God was patient with me . . . well then . . .

I sat in my patrol car, thinking about all I had learned. It was like a consuming fire in my soul. I know when I feel this way, Jesus Himself is talking to me through the Holy Spirit. The Apostle John writes of Jesus when He said:

> However, when He, the Spirit of truth, has come, He will guide you into all truth; for He will not speak on His own authority, but whatever He hears He will speak; and He will tell you things to come. He will glorify Me, for He will take of what is Mine and declare it to you. (John 16:13–14 (NKJV))

Jesus plainly declared His love for this man to me. And He wanted me to take a Scripture to him that the Holy Spirit had conveniently reminded me of in a Bible study just days before. As you're following Jesus, the Holy Spirit will show you things He wants you to learn. As the Bible says:

> But when the Father sends the Advocate as My representative—that is, the Holy Spirit—He will teach you everything and will remind you of everything I have told you. (John 14:26 (NLT))

I set my course for the hospital. I did not know what to expect when I got there. I didn't know

- whether I would be able to talk to him;

27

- if they had sedated him due to his combative nature;
- if he would just yell and curse at me as he did with everyone else; or
- if he would remember me in his drugged-out stupor.

However, the one thing I did know: Jesus reminded me that He loved Chris and needed me to reach out to him to remind him of this truth.

I walked into the emergency room and asked the charge nurse which room Chris was in and where he was being cared for. The first words out of his mouth were, "Oh, that lovely person . . . he is in Room 21."

I went around the corner. A security guard and an off-duty officer were keeping watch over him. I looked into the room; he was tied up and sleeping. The officer told me that I had just missed his ranting and yelling. He said it was nice to have him sleeping so the hallway could have some peace.

I knew I couldn't wake him up. So many times, I have been the recipient of someone working my prisoner into a frenzy and then leaving me alone with him after I had worked for so long to calm him down. I wasn't going to be *that* guy. And so, I left him sleeping, and I walked out of the emergency room.

I've got to be honest; I was a bit dejected. I wanted so badly to carry out the mission Jesus had given me—a mission to love a man who was deemed "unlovable" (at least at that moment). But I also needed to love the other people who were in the hospital and that seemed to be just as important at that point. Besides, if what the security detail said was true, I may not have even gotten a word in edgewise.

I cleared my call, and I was immediately sent to a car accident. Maybe it was all in my flesh. Maybe it wasn't from God after all. I left the parking lot to handle the accident with a burning question in my heart.

The Bible says in Isaiah:

> "For My thoughts are not your thoughts, nor are your ways My ways," says the LORD.
>
> "For as the heavens are higher than the earth, so are My ways higher than your ways, and My thoughts than your thoughts." (Isaiah 55:8–9 (NKJV))

I was trying to figure out what God's thoughts were in this case. And then I was sent back to the hospital when one of the parties involved in the accident was transported for medical reasons.

Could it be?

I finished my accident investigation and went back to check the status of my sleeping man. Chris was awake. And he was somewhat coherent. God had used the time away to clear his anger enough for me to talk to him. *This* was His way.

When I walked in to talk to him, he recognized me as the man who had prayed with him in the front yard of his house almost a year before. I told him that I had been sent by the Lord—that the Lord was still pursuing him, and Jesus still loved him. I asked him why an old cop would go out of his way to show love to him. He didn't know. I told him that it was because God had been patient with me and had saved me too. It was my heart to pass along what I knew about the love of Jesus.

Then I read him the passage Jesus had given to me for him:

> When an unclean spirit goes out of a man, he goes through dry places, seeking rest, and finds none. Then he says, "I will return to my house from which I came." And when he comes, he finds it empty, swept, and put in order. Then he goes and takes with him seven other spirits more wicked than himself, and they enter and dwell there; and the last state of that man is worse than the first. So shall it also be with this wicked generation. (Matthew 12:43–45 (NKJV))

I explained that he had cast out the unclean spirit he had been dealing with when he had found a short time of sobriety. His "house" had been put in order when he had found a job and was reading the Bible. But when he fell back into drugs, he had opened the door to his old demon and more—because he was much worse off this time than the last.

I felt compassion for him as tears welled up in his eyes. I explained that Jesus had been pursuing him for a long time, and he still had a chance to make things right. God wanted to replace what the locusts had eaten (Joel 2:25), and He wanted to show him mercy and grace.

He told me that he wanted to change . . . that he didn't want to do "this" anymore.

I laid my hands on this teary-eyed man's forehead, and I prayed for him. His drug-filled rage was gone. There was nothing left but regret for the life he had allowed to go astray.

I didn't know what Chris would do. Only God knew what he would do with the very relevant Word of God that was given to him in this season of his life. My job was only to plant seeds and water them—that is, to use my testimony and what I know of God's nature and wisdom to share the good news of Jesus Christ. It's God's duty to make those seeds grow

(1 Corinthians 3:7). If I keep myself in the Spirit, He gives me the seeds and the water, and He gives me the fields to harvest. I like that!

Even now, I still pray for Chris. His parents have become very close friends. And I continue to counsel Chris in an effort to bring him closer to the Lord.

How his story ends, only God knows. But I won't stop interceding for him in prayer; it's not in my nature. My heart is knit together with his family now.

4 / THE COMFORTER

GOD'S GRACE COMFORTS AND BINDS PEOPLE TOGETHER

RECENTLY, the Lord led me to read an article from an out-of-state newspaper. It was written almost twenty years ago and detailed how a forty-two-year-old woman was tragically killed late one night while driving her car. An object went through her windshield and struck her, causing so much internal damage that she died that night. The police made an arrest, and a twenty-year-old man was convicted for her murder.

At the time of her death, she had a daughter named Sarah who was approaching her eighteenth birthday. This tragedy was so emotionally crushing for Sarah that she never spoke about it to anyone.

God put me in contact with Sarah, who is now a middle-aged wife and mother. But the steps that led me to learn about her seldom-told story were a miracle.

In the Bible, we learn that God wants us to use the heartaches and difficulties in our past to comfort those who are hurting in the present. Consider what the Holy Spirit inspired the Apostle Paul to write:

> Blessed be the God and Father of our Lord Jesus Christ, the Father of mercies and God of all comfort, who comforts us in all our tribulation, that we may be able to comfort those who are in any trouble, with the comfort with which we ourselves are comforted by God. (2 Corinthians 1:3–4 (NKJV))

As we lean on the Lord to help us deal with the hardships in our lives, we learn how to cope. It teaches us to look for peace and healing through the mercy and grace of Jesus Christ. When we are matured through our storms and trials, we know how to help out and counsel others so they too can find Jesus, the greatest of all physicians.

I had found myself in many places to offer comfort while working as a police officer. As part of my job, I often met people for the first time in their worst possible conditions. I met Sarah in that very place.

Sarah's husband was walking her five-year-old son and infant daughter across a busy street when a turning motorist, who was unable to see them in the sun, entered the crosswalk. The baby stroller didn't get hit by the car, but it fell over and dropped the baby on the street. Besides bruising, the baby wasn't hurt. But her five-year-old brother was struck by the car and badly injured.

I still have a picture of that young boy burned in my mind, his little body lying in the street and his eyes trained on the medical personnel who were attending to him. In the hours following the accident, I learned that his heart had stopped on the way to the hospital and that he had a fractured skull, a punctured lung, and broken ribs. They were severe injuries. When I left the hospital, he was in a critical, yet stable, condition.

I had the opportunity to pray with his precious, worried parents and to pray over their son, who lay in an induced coma. My emotions were swirling within me as I watched his little body, motionless and hooked up to all that hospital equipment. Being a father myself, I couldn't imagine what they were feeling. But I knew by their hugs that I brought comfort to them in a difficult time.

Earlier, I also had the opportunity to meet the driver. She was a nurse who was headed home after a long day at work. She told me she couldn't see the crosswalk with the sun right over the trees. She drove through the family, hitting the little boy.

She immediately got out, wanting to render aid. She told me that when you're a nurse, you have vowed to help those who are in medical need. But her guilt and hurt for causing the very situation she wanted to render aid in, kept her at arm's length. The tears that streamed down her face were real. I prayed for her too.

Praise be to the Lord—the Father of all mercies and the God of all comfort. He allowed me to comfort both sides of a very serious situation.

I have learned that people aren't "calls for service." People aren't "projects." And they aren't "appointments." People are so much more than that.

Even when we clean up the scene, write the report, and put someone in jail, there are feelings, emotions, needs, and wishes that continue for those who are hurting. It is our job as Christians to walk with them for a while, to lead and guide them to peace and healing through Jesus Christ.

In Galatians, it exhorts us:

> Bear one another's burdens, and so fulfill the law of Christ. (Galatians 6:2 (NKJV))

And Jesus taught us:

> A new commandment I give to you, that you love one another; as I have loved you, that you also love one another. By this all will know that you are My disciples, if you have love for one another. (John 13:34–35 (NKJV))

So about a month later, I wanted to reach out to everyone who had been involved in the accident to see how things were going. My wife had asked me about them. And I told her that, if the week wasn't too busy, I would call them the next time I was at work.

God wants us to love people in this way, and He will even give you the opportunities to do so if you keep your eyes open. God gave me the opportunity. It was His providence that made it happen.

When I got to work on Saturday, I checked my voicemail as I always do. I had one message from a lady I didn't recognize, but she left a case number.

I don't like to get voicemails because they can be a hassle. So many times, people want me to update them on how their case is progressing. Or they want to argue with me about how they didn't like the outcome of the original case.

I was running late, so I wrote the information down, vowing to call her when I got a free minute. But the night was very busy. So, I didn't get a chance to call her.

On Sunday, I wanted to call the parents of the little boy who had been hit by the car. Unfortunately, I didn't write their names down at the time of the original call, and I couldn't remember the names of anyone involved. I knew I was going to have to do some deep research to find the case. The intersection was notorious for causing accidents, and I was not the primary officer involved in the investigation. Sunday was also busy, and I forgot to call the lady from the voicemail the day before.

On Monday, I prayed before my shift started. I asked to see something amazing, something brought on by God Himself. I prayed that He would challenge me and help me to fulfill the law of Christ in a unique and rewarding way.

When I said amen, I was immediately reminded of the voice-mail I had now neglected for two days. I checked the case number I had written down on the paper and pulled it up on my computer. It was the case number of the accident!

The report contained all the people involved and their contact information. The lady I didn't recognize on the voicemail was the at-fault driver, who had hit the little boy. I thanked the Lord for leading me to find the information I needed.

I know I could have prayed for God's help in finding the information. But God has a way of giving us the things we need even before we ask for them. Jesus Himself told us:

> For your Father knows the things you have need of before you ask Him. (Matthew 6:8 (NKJV))

The Lord knew I needed the information so I could reach out to them on His behalf. He laid it out for me to receive when it was time for me to get it. It was right on time. How amazing is our God!

So, I called the driver, and she told me she had been going through many tough things since the accident. I was able to comfort and pray for her through the love of Jesus Christ. It was truly an encouraging conversation, and one that benefited us both.

Then I called Sarah, the mother of the little boy who had been hit by the car. I learned that, miraculously, he had healed so quickly that the doctors allowed him to go home. She wanted to thank me and the other officers in the department who had been praying for his recovery. She told me this was a hard time in her life, but it was not the only difficult time she had been through.

Over the next thirty minutes, I learned about the cancer her son had survived. He had been given the "all clear" diagnosis just months before the accident. He had fought through that difficulty only to be faced with this one.

She told me how this chain of events had pulled her closer to God. She admitted that life had pulled her away from her Lord. But since her little boy had survived two heartbreaking situations, she felt that God must have huge things planned for him in the future. And she needed to bring him up in a godly home.

And then she told me something I'm still pondering to this day.

After her son woke up from a week-long coma, Sarah sat beside his hospital bed, talking to him. Her son told her that he had met her mother (his grandmother), and she told him she loved him. His mother, taken aback by the idea that he could have seen her mother, asked how he knew it was her. He told her that she looked just like her and had the same smile.

Sarah then told me about the tragic story of her mother's murder. Since her son hadn't been born until five years ago, he never had the chance to meet his grandmother. And because the pain still haunts her, Sarah never told him about her mother's death or even showed him a picture of her. After hearing this from her son, she was convinced that her mother was there to comfort him in this tough time.

Did he truly see his grandmother in heaven? Was he visited by her in his unconscious state? I don't know, but it's an incredible thought because our God can do anything.

I pray this story builds your faith and your drive to reach out to those who need comfort. If it's possible that God sent this little boy his grandmother to comfort him through his trial, then it's possible for you to reach out to those who need you, in the love and care of Jesus Christ.

5 / DON'T JUMP TO CONCLUSIONS

GOD'S GRACE GIVES US DISCERNMENT TO SEE THE TRUTH

EVERY TIME I put on my badge and uniform, I eagerly awaited what might happen during my shift. After loading up my car, I made it a habit of praying before I went out to patrol my beat. I always prayed something similar to how Moses prayed, "Please, show me Your glory" (Exodus 33:18 (NKJV)). Without fail, the Lord illustrated His personality; He always showed me His glory.

God wants loyal, available people whom He can work through. Consider what the Bible says about how God looks for people to do His work:

> For the eyes of the LORD run to and fro throughout the whole earth, to show Himself strong on behalf of those whose heart is loyal to Him. (2 Chronicles 16:9 (NKJV))

If you want the Living God to show His strength and glory in your life, you just need to be loyal to Him. And that starts with prayer.

So just like other days, I started by praying for safety and security, and for discernment and wisdom to decide the right balance between mercy and justice. After I said amen, I drove into town. Little did I know that God would show Himself strong on all of those prayer points in one call for service.

I was sent to an unknown problem where a woman had apparently been assaulted. Dispatch advised that she had blood on her face.

One thing I have learned about police work: the information you receive from dispatch isn't always what actually happened. Looking back on my career, I can remember times when I read the call notes and made a decision about what had happened and who was at fault even before I arrived. Sometimes, I even got my emotions involved in it.

But this can be foolish. The Bible even tells us:

> The first one to plead his cause seems right, until his neighbor comes and examines him. (Proverbs 18:17 (NKJV))

It's never a good idea to take the first person's story, and it's never wise to make a decision until you have as much information as you can get. Waiting for all the information is wisdom. If you don't take the initial information with a certain amount of caution, it can become very dangerous. This would be a case that showed that point.

I prayed a quick prayer while I was on my way to the call. I asked God for discernment and wisdom, so I would make the right decision. As I said before, it's a pitfall to jump to conclusions. A woman with blood on her face seems pretty cut and dry . . . until it isn't. Although I had learned over the years not to trust the call notes too much, I found myself doing exactly that. Human nature and old habits are hard to break.

I did, however, ask for God's hand of protection. Anytime physical violence is involved, you never really know if that violence might be turned on you as an officer.

When I arrived, I discovered that the woman had walked away from the fire department. This should have been caution flag number one: innocent people don't tend to walk away from help. They pointed her out as she was walking through the parking lot of the bar she had been at with a male "friend."

I approached her to find out what happened and to ask if I could help her. Domestic violence is a serious thing, and the law is clear on how I needed to proceed in these types of investigations. She started walking up the sidewalk, which borders a very busy street. To make matters worse, it had just rained, and the evening rush-hour traffic was heavy.

When I called out to her, she spun around to confront me. The call notes were correct, she indeed had blood on her face. But her behavior wasn't consistent with being a "victim." It was apparent that she had either been assaulted or injured from a fall due to her severe intoxication. (I would learn later that her blood-alcohol level was five times the legal limit.)

She didn't want help, and she didn't want to talk. This was caution flag number two. I had her calm for a moment, even in her argumentative state. But when a fireman told her that, by law, she had to be checked out in the ambulance due to her obvious alcohol intoxication and the head injury she had suffered, the season of calmness suddenly began to change.

At this point, the wheels started to fall off. I praise God and thank Him for His mercy over me in what happened next.

God is the One who gives us mercy. As David wrote in the Book of Psalms:

Because he has set his love upon Me, therefore I will deliver him; I will set him on high, because he has known My name.

He shall call upon Me, and I will answer him; I will be with him in trouble; I will deliver him and honor him.

With long life I will satisfy him, and show him My salvation. (Psalm 91:14–16 (NKJV))

After the fireman delivered the bad news that she had to be checked out, the extremely intoxicated woman yelled, "No!" and turned to run. She ran into the middle of traffic. I looked over my shoulder, but I admit that I didn't look very well. I had my eyes targeted on catching up to keep her from getting hit by a car. She stumbled in the middle of the inside lane of a very busy, three-lane street. I got to her, picked her up, and pulled her into the median.

I took a breath and thought, *Thank you, Lord.*

She flopped and struggled. But with her small stature and intoxication level, I was able to keep her under control. I was thankful that, by God's providence, the very moment we crossed the street, there was a small window of time for us to make safe passage.

Later, I was told by a fireman standing by that I had almost been run over by a box truck that was traveling way too fast for the wet street conditions. They told me I was lucky that the truck was able to slow down enough to allow me to get clear.

But I don't believe in luck.

The Bible is full of places where God is our protector . . . our shield . . . our bridge . . . our rock. As it tells us in Deuteronomy:

The beloved of the LORD shall dwell in safety by Him, Who shelters him all the day long; and he shall dwell between His shoulders. (Deuteronomy 33:12 (NKJV))

After we were able to get out of the dangers of traffic, I held her in a position where she couldn't hurt me. The ambulance pulled up next to us to provide some protection from the traffic. I tried to help her sit on the pram (an ambulance bed on wheels). But the woman put her feet on the support beam of the gurney and launched herself up in an attempt to kick at the firemen and medics who were there.

I pulled her away to keep her from hitting them before spinning her around and putting her down on the bed. I had to release her left arm so she could lay back on the pram. A struggle ensued over trying to control her right arm. In the confusion, the young lady punched me right in the mouth.

She took me by surprise, I'll give her that. It's not every day that I get punched by someone. In fact, even with years of dealing with people who would have loved to get their swings in while I was working as a police officer, I have only been punched one other time in my life.

As I said, if you jump to conclusions too quickly . . .

I'll admit it: I had this one completely wrong.

In a moment of chaos, it's hard to predict what any one person might do. Take me for example: I was not expecting this petite, young lady to punch a six-foot-two, 265-pound police officer square in the face. But It was harder to predict what happened to me as I moved to retaliate.

I spun around to attack my attacker. But the second my hands were within striking distance, I felt the Holy Spirit calm my wrath. I could feel my hard, angry face soften and my heart say, "No, Matt."

Instead of hitting her back, I just continued trying to control her hand so the medical staff could tie her hands down. I didn't even let her hateful and derogatory name-calling get to me. It was amazing! Even physical assault couldn't push me off the spiritual mark I had created through my previous environment of prayer. I was spiritually prepared to serve God and resist the devil.

It kind of reminded me of the words of the Apostle Peter:

> Be sober, be vigilant; because your adversary the devil walks about like a roaring lion, seeking whom he may devour. Resist him, steadfast in the faith, knowing that the same sufferings are experienced by your brotherhood in the world. But may the God of all grace, who called us to His eternal glory by Christ Jesus, after you have suffered a while, perfect, establish, strengthen, and settle you. To Him be the glory and the dominion forever and ever. Amen. (1 Peter 5:8–11 (NKJV))

Later on, this young lady would bite a fireman trying to render aid in the back of the ambulance. Oh, how dangerous alcohol can be—for everyone.

It's hard to show grace to someone who has hurt you. And it's hard to show grace to an enemy. But Jesus instructed us to love them. He said:

> You have heard that it was said, "You shall love your neighbor and hate your enemy." But I say to you, love your enemies, bless those who curse you, do good to those who

46

hate you, and pray for those who spitefully use you and persecute you . . . . (Matthew 5:43–44 (NKJV))

Nobody said it would be easy. Without the Holy Spirit to give us discernment, it's impossible not to want your "pound of flesh." The Spirit is our power. As the Bible says:

"Not by might nor by power, but by My Spirit," says the LORD of hosts. (Zechariah 4:6 (NKJV))

Over the last few years, I have noticed that the numbers 111 and 1111 have had a profound influence on my walk with Christ. God has used these numbers in what might be a direct sign of His direction as I follow His leading. I have to tell you how the number 111 made a difference in how I proceeded further in this case. (Stay tuned, this won't be the only time you will see these numbers.)

When I got to the hospital, I began the arduous task of deciding which crimes to charge her with. I reviewed Colorado's laws about assaulting police officers and firemen. Although the law is clearly written, my heart was troubled by what I was reading, and I needed to seek a clear answer.

Due to her violent nature, they sedated the young lady, and she was sleeping in the hospital bed. It was by chance that I looked up at her monitor and noticed that her blood pressure was 111/75. I took this as a sign to seek the Lord. I prayed for direction and was given the urge to call a lieutenant to see what he thought about the whole thing.

Most police officers are content with pressing the highest and heaviest charges on people, especially if they had been directly wronged in some way. In my old life as a police officer, I would have taken this to its highest degree. My flesh would have been inflamed, and I would have brought down "the hammer." Besides, it was my duty to punish evil-doers.

But now that I was walking with God—a new creation in Christ—I didn't feel the punishment was appropriate for the circumstances. I had recently been urged and led by the Spirit to think the best of people. If I was going to make any mistakes in my reasoning, I wanted to make them on the side of mercy. Besides, the Bible says:

> Beloved, do not avenge yourselves, but rather give place to wrath; for it is written, "Vengeance is Mine, I will repay," says the Lord. (Romans 12:19 (NKJV))

I expected that the lieutenant would throw the book at her— something, in my heart, I wasn't willing to do since she had no criminal history and no one had actually been injured. After talking to him, he advised that dropping the felony charges for lesser, misdemeanor charges was the best course of action.

Praise God that his answer was what my heart was telling me to do. I hung up with my boss and turned to see that the ambulance dropping off a patient in the bay was Ambulance 111.

The Lord wants those who seek Him to follow a very simple equation. We can see it in the Book of Micah where it is written:

> He has shown you, O man, what is good; and what does the LORD require of you but to do justly, to love mercy, and to walk humbly with your God? (Micah 6:8 (NKJV))

Seek what is right, but do it in a loving and humble manner, giving place for God to lead you in your decisions. I left the hospital feeling I had done this well.

Praise be to God that He directs my path in everything I do. I cannot imagine my life without His gentle guidance in my life. God's grace gives us discernment to see the truth.

If you want to know Him, you must pray to Him. Then, you will be able to feel His gentle hands and hear His soft voice too.

6 / THE BRIDGE

GOD'S GRACE ALWAYS BUILDS A BRIDGE

IN THE BIBLE, there is a curious verse. It says:

> The wind blows where it wishes, and you hear the sound of it, but cannot tell where it comes from and where it goes. So is everyone who is born of the Spirit. (John 3:8 (NKJV))

Jesus was telling one of the religious elites (a man named Nicodemus) that the Spirit of God works in us and through us in ways that are not fully understood. But like the wind, the Spirit will be experienced. It is this Spirit that leads us to the final destination—a meeting with the Lord Himself.

It truly amazes me how the Lord will intricately place a string of situations together to lead a believer into a meeting with Him. This happened to me one night while I was working my patrol shift. By the time I stopped to think about everything that had happened, I could only praise God for His wonderful providence.

Before we go any further, let's look at what God's providence is. We learn throughout Scripture that God has a tight grip on everything that's happening. This grip is not only on a single situation. Instead, God tracks every situation of every person, in every location throughout all of time.

It's hard to wrap your head around God's providence. But it's encouraging to know that everything happening in your life coincides with events that are happening in other people's lives to bring multiple people together to fulfill His perfect will. Think of it like the most intricate game of chess. God is moving you, a piece on the board, and He is moving others around you to work something out. Sometimes, that work is beyond belief.

My shift began by assisting a fellow officer in an investigation of a domestic dispute that started in our patrol district. It became clear that we needed to contact the guy sooner rather than later for the victim's safety.

To locate the man involved, a man we felt an urgency to arrest due to his very violent and unpredictable behavior, our investigation led us well north of our district and into a neighboring patrol district. This practice is not usually approved unless the case is important enough to leave the district. After what we had seen of the victim, we knew this case was that important.

The sergeant agreed. But all we knew was what car he was driving (including the license plate) and that he might be at his parents' house, in a mobile home park, located north of the city. It was time to go hunting; maybe the Lord would be gracious.

I drove through three mobile home parks without success. And my search took me further and further north, away from my assigned beat. I knew I would have to call off the search soon because the calls were starting to stack up in my district. But unbeknownst to me, the Lord had other plans for me, and the Spirit began to blow.

Over the radio, I heard that dispatch had sent two officers from my district to cover a call in this northern district—where I was just ending my search. This kind of dispatch only happened when the call was really labor-intensive, and the district didn't have enough officers to safely work the call.

The location of this important call was only three blocks west of where I was. I was in the area, so I took the call to free up the other cars. Needless to say, God had a plan.

When the dust settled, I found myself on the scene, in our western district, with a bunch of other officers, fire personnel, and ambulance crews. A teenage boy, who had been adopted only months before, was holding on for dear life to a light pole on the wrong side of the handrail of a bridge that spans a wide riverbed. Below him was about a fifty-foot drop where there were large and ragged rocks . . . and certain death.

The boy had jumped out of his father's car as they were going to the children's hospital to get treatment for the boy's suicidal threats. Now he was one determined act away from making those threats a reality.

I could tell by his body language that he was upset and agitated about whatever had led him to this point. Only an ambulance crewman was talking to him from a comfortable distance. However, it did not appear that he was making much headway. My initial fear was that the boy would become fatigued and let go. The tension of the moment was very high.

In my thirteen years of being a police officer, I had learned that people lean on me to make things happen and to bring situations to a conclusion. Although there were a number of officers and fire personnel there—and for all intents and purposes, I was not needed—I'll admit, pride and old habits die hard.

My thoughts went back to one thing, *What could I do to bring this kid to safety?* If God had brought me here, what would He want me to do to fix the issue? With my training in crisis intervention, my thoughts swirled around in my head about what I needed to do next.

But God . . . He almost always does something you don't expect.

At that moment, God showed me what my next job was; He chose it for me. A sergeant who was there told me she needed me to stay with the boy's father. It so happened that he was standing only a short distance away.

There are glamorous jobs on the police scene, and there are jobs that are not that glamorous. But no matter what the job is, they are all important. I was wondering what the Lord had up His sleeve because *this* wasn't how I envisioned my role, in this case, playing out. Yet, soon it would all make perfect sense.

I got into a conversation with the boy's father, and I learned that he was a believer like me. Over the next few minutes, I prayed with him (and his wife who was on speakerphone). I noticed that when I said amen, several others in the area had heard us praying, and they had laid hands on the father as well. The Bible says:

> For where two or three are gathered together in My name, I am there in the midst of them. (Matthew 18:20 (NKJV))

This tense situation was about to change. God was up to something.

I now knew why I was there. God didn't want me to talk to the boy. He had that covered. He didn't want my car to block traffic. He had that covered as well. And He didn't want me to assist the fire department; He had that covered too.

It became apparent that what God wanted was a man to stand in the gap and talk to *Him*.

And from that point on, I prayed without ceasing for the deliverance of this kid from his current mental state. I prayed that the storm in his heart would be calmed, that the raging sea in his soul would be calmed, and that he would start to remember all those who had worked tirelessly to love him. Most importantly, I prayed that God would remind him that He loved him.

At some point during this call, authorities were able to call one of the boy's friends. By the time his friend arrived to talk to him, you could see him starting to soften, and it looked like his storm was calming. A short time later, that kid, who was so desperate to end his own life, calmly stepped over the handrail, walked across the roadway, and stepped into the open arms of his friend. He got into the back of the ambulance and was whisked away to safety.

Later that night, as I was meditating on what I had witnessed, the Lord reminded me:

> [F]or through Him God created everything in the heavenly realms and on earth. He made the things we can see and the things we can't see—such as thrones, kingdoms, rulers, and authorities in the unseen world. Everything was created through Him and for Him. He existed before anything else, and He holds all creation together. (Colossians 1:16–17 (NLT))

The Lord had it covered. God had a solution, regardless of who was there. But in a world where our battles are largely spiritual ones, He wanted someone to pray. And this time, He called me.

But this wasn't the end of the story, as I would find out only a few days later.

Remember the verse I quoted at the beginning? I want to take a moment to explain it just a little more. Here is the verse again:

> The wind blows where it wishes, and you hear the sound of it, but cannot tell where it comes from and where it goes. So is everyone who is born of the Spirit. (John 3:8 (NKJV))

Although the verse, translated in English uses the word *wind*, it's important to understand that it was originally written in Greek. And, in Greek, the word *wind* in this verse, does not mean "a moving breeze."

The Greek word used in this verse is *pneuma*, which means a "life-giving spirit."[1] Jesus is referring to the Holy Spirit and His ability to move to and fro in a believer's life, making things happen in concert with God's will.

I was standing there, clearly in God's will. His providence had gotten me there. But initially, I was left searching for what God wanted me to do while I was there. That part was a little murky. I didn't think the ambulance driver was cut out for the conversation with the suicidal kid, and my pride drove me to be skeptical of his role. My skepticism changed to wonder when the ambulance driver was able to talk the kid off the bridge. I confess that my understanding of God's will in the entire situation led me to honor God when, several days later, I got the rest of the story.

I was talking to the lieutenant who was the on-scene commander that day—a good friend and a Christian. I figured it would bring him some encouragement to know that the Lord had been working behind the scenes (through His Spirit) to bring the incident to a beautiful conclusion. I didn't expect that the details I shared with him would move him to put two and two together and lead him to tell me some things I didn't know.

Earlier in that shift, while I was investigating the domestic dispute that originally led me to the area of the incident, the lieutenant had been on the scene of a traffic accident up north on a major highway toward the airport. This accident backed up traffic all the way to the off-ramp where the children's hospital is located.

An ambulance crew from a southern suburb had been traveling northbound on the highway. They were transporting a Flight for Life nurse to the airport so she could catch a flight there. When the ambulance reached the traffic snarl on the highway, created by the accident, they decided to get off on the only available off-ramp—the one that leads over the bridge to the children's hospital.

As we all have done before, they were attempting to avoid the traffic delay. And as the ambulance crossed the bridge, they found a teenager hanging on for dear life over the rocky creek bed. The crew stopped and the paramedic opened a dialogue with the despondent boy.

At the same time, a hospital police officer was crossing over the bridge, saw that something didn't look right with the ambulance, and pulled over to investigate. I learned that it is deeply frowned upon for those officers to get involved with anything "off campus." But being a veteran officer, he stopped. It was this officer who allowed clear radio traffic from the scene to my district's police dispatch because the ambulance didn't have our radio channels.

So, the Lord placed both an ambulance (who had no reason to be in that area) and a police officer (who was not to be off campus) in the right place at the right time. And then, shortly after that, the Lord placed me, way out of my patrol district, in the area as well.

But hold on . . . this story gets even better.

Earlier, I learned that the child was adopted from an Asian adoption agency in a nearby major metropolitan area. The boy's friend who arrived at the end was the adoption agent who had facilitated the adoption with his parents, the man and woman I had been praying with.

Under God's providence, the adoption agent had a relationship with the ambulance driver. At some point, the ambulance driver had adopted two Asian children through the same agency and through the same "friend."

The Lord had orchestrated a man with way more rapport than I could have ever built to talk to this kid and keep him from ending his life.

It all made sense now. God truly had it all covered.

In retrospect, I can see that, if the Lord doesn't ask me to fix the problem, there is probably a very good reason for that. I need to take a humble backseat to the action. It was apparent that God had others lined up for what He wanted to do.

In the Book of First Kings, the prophet Elijah, a man of God, ran for his life into a cave to escape from a queen who desperately wanted to kill him. When God asked him what he was doing, Elijah said:

> I have been very zealous for the LORD God of hosts; for the children of Israel have forsaken Your covenant, torn down Your altars, and killed Your prophets with the sword. *I alone am left*; and they seek to take my life. (1 Kings 19:10 (NKJV); emphasis added)

After God told Elijah not to fear and to go back and do His will, God then told Elijah:

> Yet I have reserved seven thousand in Israel, all whose knees have not bowed to Baal, and every mouth that has not kissed him. (1 Kings 19:18 (NKJV))

God has people you will never know about, waiting to be used. People like you. It's not your burden to bear. Your role is to be obedient and do whatever He asks you to do. He has a purpose for all the people involved, so the pressure is not on you alone.

As in the beginning of John 3:8, the Spirit (wind) moves where He wants. You won't know where He is going or where He is coming from. You will, however, feel Him and you will feel His effects. By the way, aren't you just amazed at how the Lord orchestrates the people on this earth, through His providence, to show His power and glory to all His creation?

If you were wondering, the Lord brought that young man to my heart a year after this happened and urged me to call the father I had prayed with on the bridge. When I did, the father told me that his son was at a special school and was flourishing under the right kind of emotional and intellectual care. Praise

God for working all things together and that the boy didn't make a rash decision during a difficult time in his life.

And one more thing. Don't despise the simple act of prayer. There is nothing more powerful you can do. Consider what the Bible says about prayer:

> Therefore I exhort first of all that supplications, prayers, intercessions, and giving of thanks be made for all men, for kings and all who are in authority, that we may lead a quiet and peaceable life in all godliness and reverence. For this is good and acceptable in the sight of God our Savior, who desires all men to be saved and to come to the knowledge of the truth. (1 Timothy 2:1–4 (NKJV))

My prayer for you, in this tumultuous time, is that you would turn your eyes toward Jesus, and that you would repent and believe in the One who sacrificed His life to save yours for all eternity. But God is a polite God, and He won't force you to do anything. Epic hurricanes, earthquakes, land-destroying wildfires, and world rulers bent on our destruction are not a judgment from God. They are a *wake-up call*.

Call upon the name of the Lord, and you will be saved. The kingdom of God is at hand!

7 / *SEE OTHERS HIGHER THAN YOURSELF*

GOD'S GRACE HELPS US TO PUT
OTHERS FIRST

I FELT HORRIBLE. It was the last day of my work week, and I was staring down another ten hours of draining and dangerous work, patrolling the streets of my city. The last three days had been a real emotional burden, and I was teetering on the idea that I needed a mental health day. I believe the saying is, "When it rains, it pours."

Not only had work been hard, I had been battling sleeplessness, financial difficulty, and physical pain. On top of that, I had received the heartbreaking news that two men I had been pouring into for the last few years had taken a turn for the worse in their fight with alcoholism, and their wives had left them, almost on the same day.

I was physically and emotionally spent. I really thought taking a mental health day was what I needed. But the Lord knew better. He had set up the day to teach me something about Himself.

I checked the calendar to see if there were enough guys on the road to cover so I could go home. No joy, we were sitting right at minimum staffing. It would take an act of God to allow me to stay home.

On the drive to work, that is exactly what I asked for—a miracle that someone else was coming to work and there had been a mistake in the staffing list. When I got there, not only were the staffing numbers at minimum, but two other officers on my shift had called in sick. This left two slots filled with guys working overtime.

I was not going home. And it was an emphatic message from God that I needed to stay. I have come to understand that those kinds of messages always lead to something magnificent in my walk with the Lord.

As I always did before my shift, I prayed that God would use me in a great way. I asked God to keep me and my co-workers safe and that we might leave the city better than we had found it at the beginning of the shift. But this prayer was a little different. I was feeling defeated and needed a lift.

We can get that lift when we wait on the Lord. In the Bible, Isaiah wrote:

> But those who wait on the LORD shall renew their strength; they shall mount up with wings like eagles, they shall run and not be weary, they shall walk and not faint. (Isaiah 40:31 (NKJV))

I have learned that if we ask in faith, and it is in God's will, He will do what we ask of Him. But I really needed some big wings to lift me up and renew my strength.

It didn't take long for the Lord to get me involved. My first call was from an elementary school. After observing the condition of a young mother picking up her kids, they were worried that she was depressed and possibly intoxicated by alcohol. They wanted us to know about it so we could investigate whether her children were in danger and whether she needed help.

I was not in the best frame of mind. Earlier that week, I had fought with one alcoholic and had been verbally berated by several others. (In fact, my first impression was that one of them might have been demon-possessed, something I seem to encounter more often these days.) It didn't help that I had poured my heart and soul into the two precious men the Lord had brought into my life, and they had fallen off the wagon hard.

Yet, the Lord had given me a heart for these people. I once had an addiction, and Jesus had set me free from it.

I was emotionally wrecked. But it was not my place to turn down the mission. I was called to render safety in the community, and this call smelled of DUI danger and child abuse. I took the call. After talking to the school staff, I pointed the nose of my patrol car toward the woman's house.

When I got there, I met the woman, named Susan, a mother of several young children. Unfortunately, the school staff had the situation pegged. Susan was "blitzed." I knew I couldn't pursue DUI charges because it was unclear what her blood alcohol level was when she was at the school. She admitted to drinking during the hour before I got to her house. But at her intoxication level, I knew with a certain degree of understanding that she had been drunk when she was driving around the busy school parking lots and picking up her kids.

Instead of condemning her on the spot for what I knew she had done—something I might have done before the Lord saved me—I asked her if she was okay. Susan burst into tears and said, "No, I'm not."

I would like to pause here and say that alcohol and drug addictions are an increasingly devastating and debilitating way for people to cope with the hardships and difficulties of life. Alcohol doesn't take away the pain. It just sweeps your pain and grief under the rug until it's time to shake the rug out. It always pops up when you least expect it, and it leads to sweeping it under the rug all over again by drinking until you forget. It's a vicious cycle. Alcoholism is not your chief problem. It is much deeper.

I heard it said once that, if we don't believe in the true place in the Bible called Hell, we make our own hell in our minds. Once we have fashioned our own hell out of paper-mache and glue, we seek to find a "god" that will keep us out of "hell."

- If your "hell" is getting fat, then the gym or a diet might be your "god."

- If your "hell" is feeling insignificant to others, then your "god" might be money, possessions, or a powerful position at work.

- If your "hell" is pain or guilt from the past, then alcohol or drugs might become your "god."

Biblically, this process is called idolatry.

Susan became a severe alcoholic after her mother died. She could never get over her mourning. In her pain, she turned to alcohol. She told me that she had tried rehab, church, and other stuff that hadn't worked.

It was her statement about church that caught my attention. I asked her more about church and then shared my own testimony of how Jesus delivered me from my own addiction. I read her the following passage of Scripture:

> The scroll of Isaiah the prophet was handed to Him [Jesus]. He unrolled the scroll and found the place where this was written:

> "The Spirit of the LORD is upon Me, for He has anointed Me to bring Good News to the poor. He has sent Me to proclaim that captives will be released, that the blind will see, that the oppressed will be set free, and that the time of the LORD's favor has come."

> He rolled up the scroll, handed it back to the attendant, and sat down. All eyes in the synagogue looked at Him intently.

> Then He began to speak to them. "The Scripture you've just heard has been fulfilled this very day!" (Luke 4:17–21 (NLT))

I explained to her that Jesus had come to cure her broken heart and release her from the bondage of alcoholism. I told her this was a promise to her if she would seek Him and get help. I then prayed over her and her family.

Susan told me that no one had ever spoken to her like that before and no one had shown interest in praying over her as I had. I explained to her that Jesus uses ordinary people, placed in extraordinary places, to reach the lost. I told her it is not her who seeks after God, but God seeks after her. I left the house after consulting with her husband about how to best pray for and support her needs.

It didn't take long for God to speak to my heart. After I climbed into the cabin of my patrol car, God told me, "It's not about you. It's not about your feelings. It's not about what you want or what you are going through. It's about Me. It's about serving Me by loving others in My name. It's about My glory."

God reminded me that, in my profession, He can insert me into places others cannot go. I love the Bible verse that says:

> And He has made My mouth like a sharp sword; in the shadow of His hand He has hidden Me, and made Me a polished shaft; in His quiver He has hidden Me.
>
> And He said to Me, "You are My servant, O Israel, in whom I will be glorified." (Isaiah 49:2–3 (NKJV))

God keeps me in His quiver to shoot me into situations and to glorify Him by His Word. Such an awesome thought . . . and an awesome responsibility. And no one has dealt with this more than Jesus did.

During the last supper with His disciples, Jesus probably had a lot on His mind. I think it was safe to say that He was "going through some stuff." He knew, in a matter of hours, He would be illegally tried as a criminal, tortured, and hung on a cross to die the most torturous death any man had ever endured.

We get some insight into what might have been on Jesus' mind in the gospel of Luke. It says:

> And He was withdrawn from them about a stone's throw, and He knelt down and prayed, saying, "Father, if it is Your will, take this cup away from Me; nevertheless not My will, but Yours, be done."

Then an angel appeared to Him from heaven, strengthening Him. And being in agony, He prayed more earnestly. Then His sweat became like great drops of blood falling down to the ground. (Luke 22:41–44 (NKJV))

The Bible is clear that Jesus knew beforehand what was going to happen. It was something so horrible that the Son of God reacted in this way when He was praying in the Garden of Gethsemane. And so, we know there was a lot on His mind.

Yet, what did Jesus do before His impending death? Look at the gospel of John:

Jesus, knowing that the Father had given all things into His hands, and that He had come from God and was going to God, rose from supper and laid aside His garments, took a towel and girded Himself. After that, He poured water into a basin and began to wash the disciples' feet, and to wipe them with the towel with which He was girded. (John 13:3–5 (NKJV))

Jesus, who was going through a lot, still served others in love by doing something that only the lowest of servants did in a Hebrew household. The Son of God and the King of kings washed another man's feet.

The lesson came full circle. God wanted me to put aside my feelings, my emotions, my physical comfort, and my laziness, so I would go to work and pray for someone who had never heard the Word of God like that before. This meant I would have to deny myself, which is exactly what Jesus said we would need to do. Jesus told His disciples:

> If anyone desires to come after Me, let him *deny himself*, and
> take up his cross *daily*, and follow Me. For whoever desires
> to save his life will lose it, but whoever loses his life for My
> sake will save it. (Luke 9:23–24 (NKJV); emphases added)

There I was, trying to stay home because I had a couple of hard
days. But the Word says I should take up my cross, *daily*, which
necessarily means some of those days when that cross is on my
shoulders will be hard ones. I started to realize that God didn't
want me lying around the house, wallowing in my own feelings. Our feelings are not always accurate, but the Word of God
is always true. And there it is—written plainly—*deny yourself*.

It is so important that we see people the way Jesus sees them.
They are not just an afterthought, set aside until we have
already taken care of our own needs. Loving people is our main
mission field (Mark 12:31). I think Paul said it well:

> Let nothing be done through selfish ambition or conceit,
> but in lowliness of mind let each esteem others better than
> himself. Let each of you look out not only for his own inter-
> ests, but also for the interests of others. (Philippians 2:3–4
> (NKJV))

God taught me that serving others is better than serving
ourselves. I learned that no matter how hard it might be, we
need to deny ourselves daily and serve the Lord and
where He has work for us to do.

And wouldn't you know it? I was lifted up on wings and
strengthened in the process! Through personal sacrifice, I
received God's grace. And you can too.

8 / FORGIVENESS—THE DUI (PART 1)

GOD'S GRACE PICKS US UP WHEN WE HAVE FALLEN

BEFORE I GO to work every day, my wife prays for me. God is faithful to deliver her heartfelt prayers. And I am thankful that I have someone in my life who walks along this road of faithful service with me.

One time, she prayed I would have an opportunity to "speak boldly in the name of Christ" to someone who needed to hear the love and encouragement only the Lord can bring. It never ceases to amaze me that, when my wife prays in faith for the Lord to use me in a specific way, He is always faithful to deliver.

The night before this spirited prayer, I had been working my patrol shift. It was a beautiful night, a wonderful change from the bitter cold and snow we had been having. I was driving around when I got a call about a traffic accident. The call notes from dispatch advised that the single-car accident was most likely due to an intoxicated driver. The car had come to rest in the parking lot of a gas station, and it appeared no one had been injured.

When I arrived on the scene, I noticed an SUV with a blown tire. All the airbags along the passenger side had been deployed.

I spoke to a witness, and I learned that the SUV had been traveling northbound in the southbound lanes of a very busy, three-lane street. The SUV had made a left turn and then cut the turn too hard while trying to get into the gas station parking lot. The SUV struck the curb with such force that the curb destroyed the tire and set off the airbags. It was miraculous that no one had been hurt.

I found a female driver and two young children in the SUV. The five-year-old boy wasn't sure exactly what had happened because of his age. But the twelve-year-old girl knew all too well what had occurred. The adrenaline was pumping, and her emotions of fear and anger were high. She was shivering uncontrollably, a feeling I have had before on several occasions when things got a little "crazy" at work.

I gave the girl my patrol jacket to keep her warm as we talked. I spoke to her about what had happened. As she told me about the scary ride she had just lived through, tears of fear started rolling down her cheeks. I felt for her so deeply that my anger started welling up inside me. How dare that woman, that intoxicated mother, put her children through this "hell."

I went over to talk to the woman while the children got into the back of an ambulance to be examined. Her name was Allison. It was obvious that Allison was heavily intoxicated by her inability to stand steady and her slurred speech. I couldn't believe that a mother in such an intoxicated state would risk the lives of herself, her kids, and the community at large so she could have a good time with her friends. My spirit burned hot.

The Bible warns us about alcohol. It says:

> Those who linger long at the wine, those who go in search of mixed wine.

Do not look on the wine when it is red, when it sparkles in the cup, when it swirls around smoothly; at the last it bites like a serpent, and stings like a viper.

Your eyes will see strange things, and your heart will utter perverse things. (Proverbs 23:30–33 (NKJV))

Over the next few hours, this lady would scream at the top of her lungs and call me all sorts of disrespectful names. Then she would flirt in an effort to get herself out of the charges she had earned, and she would complement me to gain my favor. It was clear the alcohol had done just what the Bible says.

She even tried crying to tug on my heartstrings. Tears, in an effort to sway me toward grace, have never worked on me. And they didn't work this time either. I stood by the arrest I had made, and I did not waver.

During our encounter, Allison told me that she recognized me because apparently her family and mine attend the same church. This initially did not sit well with me. I felt our mingling together in the same body of Christ could potentially open a slew of problems for me and my wife down the road.

But God always has plans for us. Even if we don't see them right away.

I got a call later that night from her husband. He had been out of town and had received a phone call from a family member, telling him that his wife had been arrested. He just wanted some answers.

I learned over the next thirty minutes that Allison was not a drinker and, when she had even half a glass of wine, she would always abstain from driving for fear of getting her family or herself killed. He told me that he was "speechless" at what he was hearing when I told him what had led to her arrest. At that moment, I started to see a picture of a woman who had made one careless decision, not someone continuing in a sinful and destructive lifestyle choice.

I told my trusted friend, a police chaplain and pastor at my church that I had arrested someone in our church for DUI. Without hesitation, he said, "Could be that God sent you to arrest her so it will get her attention better."

He led me to see the situation differently. I remembered a series of foolish decisions I had made that had led to horrible outcomes. In fact, the careless and destructive decisions that dot my past are what pulled me to trust in the Lord in my own life. As the Bible says:

> And when He [the Holy Spirit] has come, He will convict the world of sin, and of righteousness, and of judgment. (John 16:8 (NKJV))

The Holy Spirit had shown me all I had done wrong, and He had driven me to follow a righteous path. I was no better than this lady, and I knew it. My heart started to soften.

The next evening, after my wife had prayed for "boldness" in my shift, I recalled how a month earlier I had tried to help another lady, Connie, who was a severe alcoholic and suicidal. She had also called me all sorts of names. And she had said things to me that, if she had said them to me in my past, might have elicited a very angry response from me. But with the Spirit of God dwelling in me, I enjoy the fruit of being longsuffering (patience). So, I didn't let her hurtful comments get to me.

In the book, *Ministering to Problem People in Your Church*, the author made the following observation: "Don't look at them as lions. Look at them as wounded sheep."[1] When you take the ferocious "teeth" from them, you see the name-calling and hateful speech for what it is—a cry for help.

Later that week, I went back to check up on Connie. She looked at me like she had seen a ghost. She told me that she had said some mean things to me and was very sorry for hurting me. I told her that I had come to see her, hoping to meet the "real her" because I knew intoxicated, suicidal people were not themselves. I ended up ministering to and praying with Connie and her family.

This past incident stuck in my mind. I wondered if this present arrest would be a stumbling block to Allison as well. I was worried she might feel shame and embarrassment about what had happened the night before. As I was learning about leadership positions in the church, I did not want any guilt or discouragement to push her and her family away from the one place she needed to be to heal—the Church.

I asked the chaplain if it would be a good thing to "recover" Allison so she wouldn't feel the shame and hurt that might be associated with her mistakes, much like Jesus recovered Peter after Peter had denied Him just before the crucifixion (John 21:15–19). He told me that I needed to pray about it, but it seemed like a wise decision.

As I left the last call I was on, I gave the situation to the Lord. Shortly after my prayer, God gave me the most amazing feeling in my chest, a quickening of my spirit that told me He wanted me to act. As I drove several miles to their house, no calls for service came over the radio. In fact, it was the quietest it had been all shift. I parked in front of the house, and I prayed for wisdom and the message He wanted me to give.

Her husband answered the door, and I introduced myself as the officer who had talked to him the night before. He called for Allison, and she came out too. She looked horrible. I asked her how she was feeling. She told me that she felt ashamed and embarrassed. She still couldn't believe she had fallen into such a bad place. She had spent the night throwing up on a dirty floor in the detox facility I had taken her to after her arrest.

I realized she was feeling exactly like I thought she might. And I learned that this was a case of God's gift of discerning of spirits. God had given me insight into the situation to help me act in His Name.

Allison told me that she had recently been slipping away from the Church and from the Lord. It seemed the care and concern for this world had drawn her away from the grace of God. It certainly seemed to me that the chaplain was right—God might have been using me to pull her back into a right relationship with Him through difficulty and hardship. As each minute passed, I felt more and more that I had made the right decision by coming in the name of Jesus.

We see this same example in the parable of the prodigal son in Luke 15. In that parable, the son of a rich man demanded his inheritance from his father and left for a far country. By taking what was due him before his father's death, the boy was basically saying, "You're dead to me, father."

The boy took the money and squandered it until he was in a very difficult situation. The care and concern of the world had drawn him away. But now, through difficulty, he was thinking about his father. The Bible then tells us:

> But when he came to himself, he said, "How many of my
> father's hired servants have bread enough and to spare, and I

perish with hunger! I will arise and go to my father, and will say to him, 'Father, I have sinned against heaven and before you, and I am no longer worthy to be called your son. Make me like one of your hired servants.'" (Luke 15:17–19 (NKJV))

Now Allison, it appeared, had also come to the end of herself —she had come to her senses. She told me that she had repented early that morning for what she had done and she sought to be reunited with her heavenly Father.

That reminds me of the best part of the parable. If we continue reading in the Book of Luke, we learn about the father's response:

> But when he was still a great way off, his father saw him and had compassion, and ran and fell on his neck and kissed him. And the son said to him, "Father, I have sinned against heaven and in your sight, and am no longer worthy to be called your son."
>
> But the father said to his servants, "Bring out the best robe and put it on him, and put a ring on his hand and sandals on his feet. . . . for this my son was dead and is alive again; he was lost and is found." And they began to be merry. (Luke 15:20–24 (NKJV))

How powerful the message that our God, our heavenly Father, will forgive us and take us back into His grace when we return to Him.

I told Allison that I had brought her two messages from God. First, I told her that I had forgiven her. I forgave her for the things she said to me, her behavior, and her decisions. I forgave her for the danger she had put her children in and the danger to the city's citizens who had been driving on the road at that time. I told her that she had to deal with the consequences of her actions—that was not something I was going to work to take away. But I wanted her to know I held no animosity toward her if she wanted to say hello to me at church.

She told me that, when she had gotten home from detox, even her five-year-old son had told her that he had forgiven her. I told her the message, from the faith of a child, was from the Lord.

The second message, and one infinitely stronger, was that God had also forgiven her. I told Allison there was no condemnation for those who live their lives "in Christ" (Romans 8:1 (NKJV)). I explained that our God loves her, and He uses "all things" for good "to those who love" Him (Romans 8:28 (NKJV)). I told her that she needed to pull herself back to Him and allow Him to take those feelings, now in the past, away.

Like the father in the parable, God had already looked past what she had done less than a day before. And He had once again accepted her back into His grace. *That* is how powerful and compassionate our heavenly Father is toward us.

The freedom I saw in her eyes was astounding. I then prayed over them both. I asked God for restoration in their marriage and a powerful working of the Spirit in their lives. I prayed they would use their testimony to love and benefit others and to avoid the pitfalls associated with backsliding in the future.

When I said amen, her husband turned to me and said, "Thank you for being bold and for being courageous enough to come over and speak a word from the Lord."

After I left the house, I thanked the Lord for forgiving me for all I had done in my life, as I had forgiven Allison. I was blessed that God had used me to release her from the embarrassment she felt toward me and remind her that God had already released her from the condemnation she felt. The Bible says:

> If you forgive those who sin against you, your heavenly Father will forgive you. But if you refuse to forgive others, your Father will not forgive your sins. (Matthew 6:14–15 (NLT))

So, from whom are you withholding forgiveness? If you take the time to forgive them, I promise you will bring a blessing to those who are under the condemnation of your unforgiveness. And more importantly, *you* will be blessed by forgiving those whom you are holding a grudge against.

Before I said amen, I also thanked our Lord for the opportunity to *speak boldly in the name of Christ*. Prayer answered.

9 / RESTORATION—THE DUI (PART 2)

GOD'S GRACE REBUILDS OUR FAITH

MY MIND and heart had been on Allison, the young lady I had arrested for DUI several days before. I had been moved by the Spirit of God to restore her so she would not be overwhelmed by grief and condemnation.

Satan works at his best when he can bring feelings of discouragement and despair. This was what I was trying to avoid when I went, at the leading of the Spirit, to tell Allison and her husband that God had forgiven her and I didn't hold any animosity either. Our prayer circle must have been a sweet sound to the Lord.

The reality, though, was I had no control over what she or her husband would do next. After I drove my patrol car away from their house, I didn't know what would happen. Would she blow it off and continue down a spiraling path? Would she come to the end of herself and seek forgiveness . . . and maybe go back to church?

I thank the Lord that *He* knew the fruit that would come the following Sunday morning. In fact, God had been planning this meeting long before I had even met her.

The Bible says that we, as Christians, must restore those in the Church who have stumbled, those who have made mistakes (sin). In Galatians, Paul exhorted a church of believers to approach those who had sinned in a spirit of gentleness, not condemning them, so those who had faltered could feel the true and amazing grace of God. This exhortation is true even in the Church today and was the doctrine I was following when I approached her about her mistakes.

The truth is, I cannot boast about who I am because I am no better than the worst of sinners and I am no more righteous than my next decision. In fact, Galatians 6:1 (NKJV) says:

> Brethren, if a man is overtaken in any trespass, you who are spiritual restore such a one in a spirit of gentleness, considering yourself lest you also be tempted.

Paul makes it clear: be kind and gentle with those who have faltered. But make sure you humble yourself and consider your own weaknesses or you might fall as well when your pride gets the best of you.

My fear was that, if Allison felt condemnation, it would become a vice—it would become one more reason not to come back to church. It was the presence of God and loving believers that would restore her. Church was the place she needed to be the most.

Today was the beginning of a new month. With this change would come a new ministry cycle for me. The new ministry had me working in a back corner, filling coffee pots and making sure the creamer and sugar were stocked.

Normally, I don't spend any time in this part of the church, because I don't drink coffee and I like to be in the sanctuary during the service. Due to heavy renovations in our church, the coffee station was not easily visible. It was not a very glamorous job. But God can use anything we give Him for His glory.

I checked the levels of the two coffee pots. When I turned to look down the hall, Allison and her husband were standing there. He had a big smile on his face as he reached to shake my hand. I could feel her nervousness as she walked up to me. I shook her hand, gave her a warm smile, and offered them both a cup of coffee.

We talked for a short time about how they were doing. I told them that I was glad to see them. Allison told me the first face she saw as she walked in the front door and toward the coffee pot was mine.

I told her it was not a coincidence.

Sometimes, God works in direct ways to make His will a reality. We can see that in the miracles He did throughout the Scriptures. For example, Jesus directly healed two blind men. In the Bible, we read:

> So Jesus stood still and called them, and said, "What do you want Me to do for you?"

> They said to Him, "Lord, that our eyes may be opened." So Jesus had compassion and touched their eyes. And immediately their eyes received sight, and they followed Him. (Matthew 20:32–33 (NKJV))

At other times, God uses indirect methods to bring His will to pass. This is called God's providence. We can define *providence* as: "God conceived as the power sustaining and guiding human destiny."[1] In other words, God has the ability to work everything together to bring about a certain outcome.

A good example of God's providence is the story of the woman at the well in John 4. It was God's providence for Jesus to walk through Samaria, a city where the Jews didn't dare go, so He would meet a woman (and a city) in desperate need of His saving grace. We read:

> The woman then left her waterpot, went her way into the city, and said to the men, "Come, see a Man who told me all things that I ever did. Could this be the Christ?" Then they went out of the city and came to Him. (John 4:28–30 (NKJV))

And a little later:

> And many of the Samaritans of that city believed in Him because of the word of the woman who testified, "He told me all that I ever did." So when the Samaritans had come to Him, they urged Him to stay with them; and He stayed there two days. And many more believed because of His own word.
>
> Then they said to the woman, "Now we believe, not because of what you said, for we ourselves have heard Him and we know that this is indeed the Christ, the Savior of the world." (John 4:39–42 (NKJV))

Jesus used a "chance" meeting with a woman who had a questionable past, to preach the gospel to a city that would not have been given the opportunity because of its "tarnished" reputation with the Jews. That was God's providence, His invisible hand at work for His glory.

In our case, I was standing in the right place at the right time so Allison would run into me, at the very place where she was going . . . the coffee station.

They sat down for the service—the first church service she had been to in almost a year—and God's providence continued. The message was about the grace of God—how striving to "do good" in our own strength, outside God's loving grace, is impossible and only leads to exhaustion and despair.

It was as if God had given her a ticket for a special showing of *What God Needs to Say to Me Today*. If I hadn't been the recipient of that very same "special engagement ticket" for my life, I would not have believed it. But I have learned that God works in ways I could have never expected.

Here was a woman who had made a monumental mistake when she was arrested for DUI, one that brought her to a place of humility she hadn't been to before. Her indiscretion brought me into the picture, and God pushed me to speak a word into her life with courage and power. I guess the text message I got from the police chaplain was right. God had used her arrest to get her attention.

But the story gets even better.

In First Corinthians 5, Paul wrote to the church in Corinth about a man who was having a sexual relationship with his stepmother. Paul told the church to take disciplinary action against him:

> In the name of our Lord Jesus Christ, when you are gathered together, along with my spirit, with the power of our Lord Jesus Christ, deliver such a one to Satan for the

destruction of the flesh, that his spirit may be saved in the day of the Lord Jesus. (1 Corinthians 5:4–5 (NKJV))

Paul was telling the church to expel him from their congregation until he repented of his sins and came back a new man, free from the bondage of sexual immorality. Although this story is specific to this church and to this one sin, we can infer that the Lord will bring about discipline to bring you back to righteousness in Him.

In fact, we read in Hebrews:

> No discipline is enjoyable while it is happening—it's painful! But afterward there will be a peaceful harvest of right living for those who are trained in this way. (Hebrews 12:11 (NLT))

There was no doubt that Allison was disciplined by God for her actions. I hoped she would repent and draw near to the Lord for strength. This outcome had yet to be seen. But we must act in gentleness to recover and repair those who have fallen, in an effort to keep them on the right track.

Consider Paul's change of heart in the second letter to the church in Corinth:

> This punishment which was inflicted by the majority is sufficient for such a man, so that, on the contrary, you ought rather to forgive and comfort him, lest perhaps such a one be swallowed up with too much sorrow. Therefore I urge you to reaffirm your love to him. (2 Corinthians 2:6–8 (NKJV))

Paul had received word that the church had expelled the man just as he had asked. But in hearing the man had repented and changed his ways, Paul called for the church to pull him back into the church in love, so he would not be left out and fall into despair and sorrow, the very trap Satan sets in our lives.

My wife, who has the tremendous spiritual gift of mercy, knows all about the calls I go on. She is a great support to me and has a heart for the people I minister to. I pointed Allison and her husband out to her, telling her about the amazing faithfulness of God earlier in the morning.

My wife got up and walked up to Allison and introduced herself. I watched my loving wife hold her in an embrace for no less than five minutes as tears streamed down Allison's face. I cannot explain the heart she has for hurting women. It was a beautiful picture of what Paul was talking about—"restor[ing] such a one in a spirit of gentleness" (Galatians 6:1 (NKJV)).

And it was a true and accurate mosaic of the grace of God, through the sacrifice of our Lord Jesus Christ. When we were condemned as sinners, there was no way to get ourselves back into good standing with God based on our good behavior. The Bible tells us that even one mistake, one sin, leaves us dreadfully short of the level of righteousness needed to have a relationship with God. But Romans 8 says:

> The law of Moses was unable to save us because of the weakness of our sinful nature. So God did what the law could not do. He sent His own Son in a body like the bodies we sinners have. And in that body God declared an end to sin's control over us by giving His Son as a sacrifice for our sins. He did this so that the just requirement of the law would be

fully satisfied for us, who no longer follow our sinful nature
but instead follow the Spirit. (Romans 8:3–4 (NLT))

Simply put, you cannot be pure enough and good enough in
your own behavior to pay the debt you owe to God by sinning.
But because God loves you so much and wants you to be with
Him, He sent His Son, Jesus Christ, to pay for your debt so
you would be debt-free in His eyes. Since that debt to God
requires payment with your life, Jesus had to die to fulfill that
debt. What a glorious truth!

And even now, as I review this story several years later, Allison
and her family still bless the walls of the church. She has
become a good friend to my wife. My wife has discipled her
through the tremendous highs of having another child and the
crushing lows of her brother dying suddenly. Through it all,
the fruit of God's grace has been shown in all kinds of ways.
God is amazing!

10 / A BRAZEN ATTACK

GOD'S GRACE STRENGTHENS US IN THE STORM

I LOVE THANKSGIVING. It is awesome to take stock of all you are thankful for. And it's always a good idea to voice those blessings to those you love.

Although I'm thankful for my family and friends and the blessings I have, I wish to highlight something else for which I am grateful. And it's something that might come wrapped in a different kind of package.

I am thankful I serve the God of the second chance. As sinners —prideful and arrogant people—we don't deserve a second chance. But the Bible says:

> This I recall to my mind, therefore I have hope.

> Through the LORD's mercies we are not consumed, because His compassions fail not. They are new every morning; great is Your faithfulness. "The LORD is my portion," says my soul, "Therefore I hope in Him." (Lamentations 3:21–24 (NKJV))

God's mercies are new *every* morning. As famous poet and author Maya Angelou said, "This is a wonderful day. I've never seen this one before."[1] It's easy to read this quote and gloss over it in passing . . . until you have one of those days that stops you in your tracks. Then you will look at this quote a little differently.

After working as a police officer for fifteen years, I had seen a lot of difficult stuff. But nothing could prepare me for what I saw that day.

As is my custom (like Daniel in Daniel 6:10), I pray for my shift and for the men and women who serve—that we may come home safely. I always ask God, as Moses did in Exodus 33:18 (NKJV), to "show me Your glory." There are very few times after praying this that I do not behold something amazing in God's plan for my shift. However, the glory God would show me on this night would take some time for me to comprehend.

The Lord had given me the charge of checking up on a man named Jeff, whom I had come to admire during my time on the beat. The old Navy vet had been through many things in his eighty years on this earth: three wars, sinking ships, dramatic storms at sea, and severe health issues. And he has been such a blessing to me. While I was praying with Jeff, a call for a "home invasion robbery" came over the radio.

The call itself didn't catch me by surprise. With the increase of "in-home" marijuana growth and production, home invasion robberies have been happening more and more often. It also didn't catch me off guard that the homeowner had been "injured" (home invasions are violent). Since it was not in my beat and there were already several officers going, I continued my ministry with Jeff.

The two responding officers got to the house, and it was quickly apparent in their voices and their requests that this was not your normal home-invasion call. In fact, I would learn later that it was not a home invasion at all, but a calculated attack. They needed another officer to respond.

Ministering to Jeff had placed me just a few blocks away, so I said amen and goodbye to him. I hurried over and got there in time to see the paramedics loading the victim into the back of an ambulance. The officers on the scene said they needed my help clearing the house to make sure the suspect was not still there and then to follow the ambulance to the hospital. They told me the victim was in bad shape and they were not able to get any information from her.

The house was a mess. There was blood everywhere. It appeared a severe struggle—maybe even a life-and-death one—had occurred inside the house. All we knew at the time was someone who had arrived there had assaulted the female home-owner. When it was safe, I left to follow the ambulance.

Shortly after we departed, the ambulance driver turned on the lights and sirens. This wasn't a good sign as it meant the patient's condition was deteriorating. I also turned on my lights and sirens. Because I was in a faster and more maneuver-able vehicle, I took up positions in the intersections in front of the ambulance so the traffic would be stopped when the ambulance got to me. This made it possible for the ambulance to continue on its path to the hospital, unhindered by stoplights and traffic.

They took the patient into Trauma Room 1—the room reserved for the most severe of situations. It was then that I got to see the patient, a woman so badly beaten I could not tell you what she looked like normally.

This was the way Jesus looked when He was crucified. In the Book of Isaiah, it tells us:

> But many were amazed when they saw Him. His face was so disfigured He seemed hardly human, and from His appearance, one would scarcely know He was a man. (Isaiah 52:14 (NLT))

Until you have seen someone in that state, it is hard to render the sight in your imagination.

But the Russian woman, whose name was Alice, was awake and alert. Although she was in pain, she clearly and precisely told me what had happened with incredible detail.

Two years before, she had been working with a psychiatric patient. When he knocked on the door, she was surprised to see him through the peephole since so much time had passed. After Alice opened the door, "the patient" attacked her with the claw side of a hammer.

His attack broke both of her arms, the bones around her right eye and other parts of her face, and fractured her forehead in three places, so deep, any one of them could have (and probably should have) killed her. She was able to will herself up the stairs and out the front door to her neighbor's house where they called 911.

I have seen wickedness in many forms, but this one shook me to the core. Considering the timing, the mental status, and how the attacker had planned this out, I'm convinced it was demonic in nature. I am also convinced God put me there for exactly the opposite reason. God had a plan . . .

A lot of people at the hospital kept saying, "She is lucky." But I don't believe in luck. Because of that, I could confidently tell Alice it was not by luck she was alive (as the doctors were saying). I told her that God had her in His hands and He apparently wanted her alive—He had given her a second chance. I told her that I would pray for her as they wheeled her into surgery.

While I was at the hospital (and in the quietness of my mind amidst the chaos), I prayed the attacker's sin would very quickly find him out. That prayer was answered too. The suspect was apprehended in short order and put in jail, even though he had fled to another city. Thank God that the man's demonic terror was over. Thank the Lord that He is gracious to hear our prayers.

I didn't see Alice again that night. After getting off shift, I went home. But I could not sleep. The snapshots I had taken in my mind of her badly beaten and bloodied face and the echoes of her painful moans continued to pass through my thoughts and dreams. I think I got a glimpse of what acute post-traumatic stress disorder feels like, and it was hell. I was so angry at what he had done to her.

In my sleeplessness, I opened the Bible to find solace in God's Word. I came across the following verse:

> Be angry, and do not sin. Meditate within your heart on your bed, and be still. (Psalm 4:4 (NKJV))

I know some of my anger was righteous but some of it was fury. Fury and wrath are sinful, and I needed to relieve their poison in my mind. I decided that I needed a "second chance."

I needed another picture of Alice in my head so I could dwell on better days. I prayed to the Lord for an open door to see her again. I hoped with a better "picture" I could alleviate the anger I felt.

As we saw in Lamentations 3:22–23, God's mercies are new every morning. And His mercies were new for me too.

Two days later, I was back on the street. And the Lord graciously gave me a window of time when calls for service had stopped. I paid Alice a visit in the hospital, and I learned a very valuable (and heart-healing) lesson.

Alice, a believer in Christ, was not bitter. She was not hateful toward her attacker. Instead, she was thankful for what the police and fire department had done. She was grateful for her neighbor, even though they had been at odds for months over an issue with his trashcans. She said, in her weakened state, she could not make it across the street to her friend and had to go to his house despite the strained relationship. To her surprise, he came out, called 911, and held her until paramedics arrived. It seemed even that relationship was given a "second chance."

It's impossible to be thankful and bitter at the same time. Her inner strength was amazing. After defeating cancer, she had survived this too. She truly believed God was the only One to be thinking about in this matter. And she was thankful for the "second chance."

To my amazement, she only had some stitches on her forehead that hid the gashes I had seen several days before. The swelling of her eye had diminished completely, and she looked so much better. I was truly and graciously given a "second chance" to see her and who she really was. Now my mind and my heart could rest—and I could meditate on the goodness of God instead of the anger of my flesh.

I prayed with her before leaving the hospital. Then I spent the next few hours meditating on God's goodness and faithfulness.

I am truly thankful for a God who gives second chances and the glory and honor that come from truly trusting in His presence in all situations. This would be cemented in my mind the next time I spoke to her.

Ten days later, I had the opportunity to visit Alice. She had recovered enough from her injuries and surgeries that she was allowed to head back to the place where this great trial had begun . . . her home.

I had waited patiently until the day God might bless me with a chance to serve her again. My shift started as it always did; I prayed God would show His glory to me. I also prayed, if it was in His will, I would have the opportunity to meet with Alice. I didn't expect that both prayer requests would be thoroughly and definitively answered at the same address, at the same time.

Alice was in good spirits, and we talked about how she was recovering. It was a miracle in itself that, despite the stitches and staples, she had full use of her hands and wrists. A prolific knitter, she showed me that she had knitted one row across on a scarf that day. This was half a row better than a few days before when she had tried without success.

She told me about her ultra-paranoid fears of being alone in the house where her life was almost taken from her. Every small noise caused her to panic just a little. Her neighbors had all pulled together to support her. And that included the alcoholic neighbor who had accused her of stealing his trash cans—the one who had graciously put away his prejudices to call 911 and comfort her while they waited for help to arrive. She has a better relationship now with all of them, but especially him because he checks up on her from time to time. She shared how she had fought off a very difficult bout with cancer several years ago, and how God had blessed her to be cancer-free for the last two years.

It was a blessing when she told me how much the incident had changed the way she looked at and cared for other people. Like many others who have near-death experiences, she had a new lease on life. And she intended to make it count for others. She gave glory to God for the way He was working in the good and the bad in her life.

I reminded her of Romans 8:28 (NKJV):

> And we know that all things work together for good to those who love God, to those who are the called according to His purpose.

It probably goes without saying that for the above verse to work best, time and testing must be in focus. That is, patience is a virtue in this kind of work. Good things and bad things must have time to happen and be knitted together cohesively for God to use them in our lives. Time must pass. We must have the patience to truly bear fruit in those times. But what Alice told me next, just about knocked me off my feet.

About thirty years ago, while she was still living in her home country of Russia, she learned something peculiar about herself. It's no secret that Russia is cold. To keep your head warm, you must have a warm hat. She explained that the warm hats had to be custom-fitted to the size of your head because the animal skins don't stretch. She laughed as she told me that Americans make fun of Russians for the hats they wear. She said Russians don't care what we think because the hats they wear are warm.

One cold day, her custom fur hat didn't fit her head anymore. She couldn't understand why it would not pull down to her ears as it once did and why it seemed to sit on top of her head like a pencil eraser. She was an adult and her head had not changed measurements in years. She was worried there was something medically wrong in her head. Fearing cancer, tumors, and deformities in her skull, she sought medical help for her condition.

Her doctor x-rayed her skull and brain. There were no tumors or other significant issues. But the bones on her forehead and the top of her skull had grown abnormally thick. It wasn't an issue of concern; it was just a genetic anomaly.

Relieved at the prognosis, she went on with her life and forgot all about it. Interestingly enough, Alice and her doctors believe it was the extra thick bone structure in her skull that withstood the punishing blows from the hammer that should have killed her.

After I prayed with her about the glory of the God we both serve, I left her house to move on to other calls. The next call was an unrelated, minor traffic accident. One of the people involved was an elderly woman named Betty. The crash had shaken her up pretty badly, so she chose an ambulance ride to the hospital.

When the accident scene had been cleaned up, I went to the hospital to meet with Betty. She told me this was not her first accident. She had been in a traffic accident so serious she was almost pronounced dead on the scene. They chose to transport her to the hospital to give her a second chance. On that ride to the hospital, they got her vitals back.

Betty had been in a coma for almost a week. Then they fought to save her badly crushed, left leg. The doctors told her there was no guarantee they would be able to save her leg. Facing the possibility of having her leg amputated and the idea that she might never walk again, she was understandably demoralized. I noticed she still had her left leg, and she told me that she had relearned to walk in a little under six months.

I was blessed to hear about Betty's story of survival. And I told her what I had learned about Alice less than an hour before—how she had been severely beaten with a hammer and how God had saved her life too.

The technician, who was in the room getting ready to wheel Betty out to get a CAT scan, remembered doing the CAT scan for Alice the night she was assaulted. She told me that due to her head injuries, Alice had died on the table before being revived by the doctors. She was blessed to hear that Alice had recovered well considering the injuries she had observed.

The power of God's sovereign healing hand and His immutable (unchanging) will are evident in the miracles in both Alice's and Betty's lives.

After I left the hospital, I got to thinking: the most desperate incident in Alice's life happened in an instant. The suspect knocked on the door, she opened the door, and sudden terror fell upon her. But by God's grace, she survived the brutal assault.

Alice physically stood before me as a testament to the following passage:

> He shall cover you with His feathers, and under His wings you shall take refuge; His truth shall be your shield and buckler. You shall not be afraid of the terror by night, nor of the arrow that flies by day. (Psalm 91:4–5 (NKJV))

She had been shielded and protected from death because God had a plan for her. And God has a plan for us all. He cares deeply about His children. As the psalmist said:

> Precious in the sight of the LORD is the death of His saints. (Psalm 116:15 (NKJV))

This verse shows that God values the timing and manner of the death of each of His children. God will not allow a believer to die without there being maximum value and benefit to His kingdom.

And this thought cannot be illustrated any better than in this case. Although Alice's life was almost taken by the hands of a demonic attack against her, God didn't allow her to die. There would have been no value to His kingdom in her death.

Instead, by His sovereignty, God put His own plan into action . . . thirty years before the incident when He thickened Alice's skull. The Lord set a defense against the attack by physically thickening her skull bones so Satan's hammer attack would not prevail.

This brings me tremendous encouragement. When I think things are falling apart in an immediate and dramatic instant in my life, God has most likely been planning against it for some time, maybe even years before the fact. It's truly possible that God has been moving mountains outside my vision, getting me ready for the instant of time when I recognize the problem. When you look at it this way, sudden terror is not so sudden. It makes it easier to see God's hand in the plan.

The Bible demonstrates how God works beforehand, over long periods of time, so His perfect plan is accomplished in men's lives.

For example, Noah started building the ark when God told him to—120 years before the judgment of the flood killed every living thing that was on the earth. The storm was sudden and deadly to those who didn't believe Noah's warning. But God had been planning it ahead of time . . . at least as long as it took Noah to build the ark. The Bible says:

> And God said to Noah, "The end of all flesh has come before Me, for the earth is filled with violence through them; and behold, I will destroy them with the earth.
>
> Make yourself an ark of gopherwood; make rooms in the ark, and cover it inside and outside with pitch." (Genesis 6:13–14 (NKJV))

We see another example in the life of Moses. Moses lived for forty years on the back side of the desert as a lonely shepherd. God painstakingly developed and humbled him over that time, so he could lead and save His people. God's will in Moses's life was to deliver the children of Israel from the bondage of Egypt. God's calling upon his life, through the burning bush, was an incident that occurred in an immediate manner. Yet, God had been molding Moses for much longer.

Joseph spent two years in prison after he interpreted the dreams of the chief baker and the chief butler before he was released to change the direction of Egypt forever. The seven years of plenty and the seven years of famine were coming. But it was not yet time to hear God's plan through Joseph. The Bible tells us: "Then it came to pass, at the end of two full years, that Pharaoh had a dream . . . ." (Genesis 41:1 (NKJV)). The opportunity for Joseph to interpret Pharaoh's dream was an immediate change in Joseph's situation. But God had been molding him in prison for far longer than that.

And finally, we learn in the New Testament that God had allowed a man to be blind since birth. The story, found in John 9, shows that God allowed the blindness in the man's life to continue into his adult years so His glory could be witnessed in an instant. Jesus told the Jewish rulers, "Neither this man nor his parents sinned, but that the works of God should be revealed in him" (John 9:3 (NKJV)).

Alice's case was similar to this blind man's story. God had used and developed Alice's body, over years of time, to glorify His name in her survival. Then those who saw God's glory could witness and praise Him continuously. In Alice's survival, God's glory was revealed, and His kingdom was furthered.

Stories like these illustrate how important patience is when you're seeking God's will for your life. You can trust God and be patient, even when you have no idea what God is doing behind the scenes. He is working for you and developing you. It is true what the Book of Philippians says: you can be confident because "He who has begun a good work in you will complete it until the day of Jesus Christ" (Philippians 1:6 (NKJV)).

Like a fruit tree revealing its harvest, it doesn't happen overnight. It takes time. I have always believed things that occur in a short period of time won't have the quality to last. But if you hold fast to the God of the universe, He will patiently shape you and mold you into the image of Christ. At that moment, He will have completed the good work He has started in you.

Let's praise God for His work in our lives, and the wisdom to see His hand in everything!

11 / THE WANDERING GRANDMA

GOD'S GRACE HAS A PLAN OF ACTION

RECENTLY, I read the following quote:

> Those who leave everything in God's hand, will eventually see God's hand in everything.[1]

The author, who is unknown, must have had a walk with God that had become so intimate, that even the simple, ordinary stuff in his or her life had obvious, observable, and divine purpose.

In my day-to-day work as a police officer, I too had come to see that the hand of God is always working to put me into the center of His will. I want to tell you about one such incident. But first, I need to tell you a story . . . a Bible story.

Before Saul was anointed king of Israel, he worked around his father's house. In First Samuel, we learn that the donkeys that belonged to his father's estate had wandered off into the wilderness and were lost (1 Samuel 9:3). So, Saul's father gave him instructions.

> And Kish said to his son Saul, "Please take one of the servants with you, and arise, go and look for the donkeys."
> (1 Samuel 9:3 (NKJV))

Saul lived in a very wealthy family. It's probably fair to say that there were many servants to tend to the issues on the estate. But Saul's father asked his son to go look for the lost donkeys himself.

It's probably also a good bet that Saul was not particularly happy with his father's request. However, we read that Saul was obedient to his father. The next few verses explain that Saul left to do the menial task of trying to find these donkeys. And for all intents and purposes, Saul did a very thorough and diligent job looking for them.

But unbeknownst to Saul, in another part of Israel, God had been speaking to His prophet, Samuel, about His choice for the first king of Israel. God had already started the task of putting the puzzle pieces together—pieces that would ultimately cause the prophet Samuel and the young Saul to meet.

As we continue reading, we see that God's much grander plan for Saul's life was starting to take shape.

> And he [Saul] said to him [his servant], "Look now, there is in this city a man of God, and he is an honorable man; all that he says surely comes to pass. So let us go there; perhaps he can show us the way that we should go." (1 Samuel 9:6 (NKJV))

Saul needed advice, and he was about to come face to face with the prophet Samuel. Saul needed to find his donkeys. But

Samuel needed Saul for a much greater purpose—to anoint him king of Israel. The Bible tells us:

> Now the LORD had told Samuel in his ear the day before Saul came, saying, "Tomorrow about this time I will send you a man from the land of Benjamin, and you shall anoint him commander over My people Israel, that he may save My people from the hand of the Philistines; for I have looked upon My people, because their cry has come to Me."
>
> So when Samuel saw Saul, the LORD said to him, "There he is, the man of whom I spoke to you. This one shall reign over My people." (1 Samuel 9:15–17 (NKJV))

As the story continues, Saul is anointed as the first king of Israel, and King Saul delivers God's people from the Philistines. This historical event started when God used something very ordinary—some wandering donkeys and several obedient men to complete the puzzle of His will.

Now, my heart has always been to show how the true stories in the Bible can come to life in this current time. I want you to see how relevant the Word of God actually is. I want to tell you the same story again. Only this time, there were no wandering donkeys. There was only a "wandering grandma."

One January, I was working patrol on a chilly, winter night. I was called to a certain residence to make a missing person's report for an elderly woman who had wandered off. It was there that I met her daughter, Mary. She was worried sick that her mother, Nora, who was eighty-six years old and suffering from dementia, had gotten lost.

We located Nora several hours later. She had walked for about five miles. It was a relief to get her home safely.

This was not the first time Nora had wandered off. Now that I was familiar with her, I was diligent in looking for her when I heard her name come across pending calls for service. Over the next three and a half years, I found Nora three more times and took her home.

We receive missing person calls all the time, and it's a normal, mundane call for a patrol officer. So, how could I have known that God had a much deeper reason for this wandering woman in my life . . . and in the lives of her family?

The third and final time I brought Nora home was in the spring, three years later. When I got her there, I learned Mary had recently been diagnosed as terminally ill. She told me that she didn't have the strength to stop her mother from leaving the house anymore and needed some advice on what to do.

We discussed the options, which were few, but we did the best we could. In our conversation, I got a distinct feeling that Mary and her "wandering" mother were both Christians. She happily accepted my invitation to pray with them over the situation and her deteriorating health.

When I left, I felt that was the last of it. But God is always working behind the scenes. If you aren't listening for His voice in the simple things of life, you might miss out on the real reason God has you there in the first place.

Several days later, I was working my shift, and I felt a strong movement of the Spirit in my heart to go back and pray over Mary again. It had been a busy day, and my shift was coming to an end. There were plenty of reasons I shouldn't have gone to the residence. But I have learned when God instructs us to do something, He doesn't change His mind.

To make it harder, what I felt the Lord calling me to do was pretty bold in that it wasn't just a prayer of healing but an anointing of oil as instructed in James. The Bible tells us:

> Is anyone among you suffering? Let him pray. Is anyone cheerful? Let him sing psalms. Is anyone among you sick? Let him call for the elders of the church, and let them pray over him, anointing him with oil in the name of the Lord. And the prayer of faith will save the sick, and the Lord will raise him up. And if he has committed sins, he will be forgiven. (James 5:13–15 (NKJV))

I pulled into the parking lot of the apartment complex hoping, at this late hour, the lights to the apartment would be turned off for the night. To my genuine surprise, everyone appeared to be awake.

I knocked on the door, and I was greeted by Nora and Mary's boyfriend. They warmly invited me inside. I found Mary sitting at the kitchen table. I'm sure all three of them were curious about why I was there since they had not called this time.

I explained God's leading in my heart—how God, through His Spirit, had urged me to use anointing oil on the sick. Without objection, I anointed Mary's forehead with oil. The four of us prayed for healing and the state of their household. I was told she only had about six months to live. I assured them that I would keep them in my prayers. I left the apartment, drove back to the precinct, and went home for the night.

On Easter Sunday later that month, I again felt a stirring in my heart for Mary and her sickness. This time, it was an even bolder move as the Spirit wanted me to take communion to her and anyone else who was there. I had developed the feeling that, in her weakened state, she probably couldn't go to church.

I finally was able to get to her house two days after Easter. God had made it clear to me that He wasn't going to change His mind. The revelation of God's steadfastness in His leading was important because He had asked me to read a passage of Scripture that was somewhat adventurous in its teachings. I had been hesitant to take it to Mary. But God wanted obedience, and I could not disobey Him.

I read the following, familiar passage of Scripture about communion:

> For I received from the Lord that which I also delivered to you: that the Lord Jesus on the same night in which He was betrayed took bread; and when He had given thanks, He broke it and said, "Take, eat; this is My body which is broken for you; do this in remembrance of Me." In the same manner He also took the cup after supper, saying, "This cup is the new covenant in My blood. This do, as often as you drink it, in remembrance of Me."
>
> For as often as you eat this bread and drink this cup, you proclaim the Lord's death till He comes. (1 Corinthians 11:23–26 (NKJV))

Most pastors only read verses 23 through 26, which is Paul's explanation of the Lord's supper. But the Lord wanted me to continue through the next few verses.

> Therefore whoever eats this bread or drinks this cup of the Lord in an unworthy manner will be guilty of the body and

blood of the Lord. But let a man examine himself, and so let him eat of the bread and drink of the cup. For he who eats and drinks in an unworthy manner eats and drinks judgment to himself, not discerning the Lord's body. For this reason many are weak and sick among you, and many sleep. For if we would judge ourselves, we would not be judged. But when we are judged, we are chastened by the Lord, that we may not be condemned with the world. (1 Corinthians 11:27–32 (NKJV))

This was a bold statement to make to someone who is sick. I didn't know Mary well enough to be this bold. But I wanted to make sure she didn't have any unrepented sins or roots of bitterness that would defile the communion table I had brought to her. I was happy to hear she had forgiven and forgotten, and she had repented and turned away from the alcohol that had ravaged her life in times past. Mary, Nora, and I took communion together. And then we prayed.

This was the last time God placed Mary on my heart. I felt the Lord was finished with me as far as Mary and Nora were concerned. But God had only stopped using me for a short time while He worked out some other things in Mary's life.

God is *never* done with us.

On a Saturday, near the end of May, I received a voicemail from Mary's boyfriend saying things had taken a turn for the worse. I had crossed his mind as a man who had a spiritual connection with his girlfriend. And he asked for copious amounts of prayer. In an instant, God had me back in the picture.

I learned when I called him back that Mary had suffered a massive heart attack, and she was clinging to life in an ICU hospital bed. I was working on shift, but I was given permission to make a hospital visit to comfort and pray over her. Mary's boyfriend and two grown children were in the room. I left the room with a heaviness in my heart. But I was blessed God had allowed me into such an intimate and difficult family space.

Over the next two days, things got worse for Mary. I had kept in contact with her boyfriend. He informed me that they were trying to make her comfortable because she only had a few days to live. He had a power of attorney over her medical decisions, and he was not sure what to do. The doctors were telling him that his loving girlfriend was suffering and had no way of recovering. They told him to let her go and turn off the machines. But he didn't want to rule out a miracle from God.

I told him that I would come to pray with him about the decision. I was again given favor by my sergeant, and I made another hospital visit. This time it was just her boyfriend and me. He told me that her heart was only functioning at five percent of its capability, and there was too much damage to her heart.

We prayed together that the Lord's will would be done, and that God would take the decision out of his hands—that God would either take Mary home to be with Him or heal her in a miraculous way. After I prayed, I left the hospital to finish my shift.

The following morning, one glorious morning later, at 0700 hours, her heart finally gave out. And she peacefully passed away.

It was fitting that her final day on Earth would end at 0700 hours on the dot, seven being the Biblical number of completion and perfection. God knows the day you will complete your time on Earth. The Bible tells us:

> Your eyes saw my substance, being yet unformed. And in Your book they all were written, the days fashioned for me, when as yet there were none of them. (Psalm 139:16 (NKJV))

The days fashioned for His loving daughter had come to a close. Now Mary is in the presence of her beloved Father and our Lord, Jesus Christ.

It's crazy to think the Lord had used a "wandering grandma" to bring a listening servant into a sick woman's life. It's a tremendous honor, but heavy at the same time, that God used me over those few interactions to make sure everything was prepared for her departure.

I learned during this time that, shortly after I prayed with them and anointed her with oil, Mary and her boyfriend took the steps to get her house in order. It wasn't something they had ever thought about or talked about before. It was this discussion that gave power of attorney to the one who would ultimately be standing by her side when that very real decision came.

But God gives "grace for grace" (John 1:16 (NKJV)), and he didn't have to make that decision after all. There is no doubt in my mind Mary's heart is with the Lord. She proved that over the times we discussed Scripture and prayed. I felt she hadn't been holding on to any bitterness or unrepented sin as we took a final communion. And I felt she had truly accepted Jesus as her Savior. There is no doubt she is in the glorious presence of Jesus Christ now . . . and for eternity.

I had no idea all of this would be the final outcome when I went to find a wandering woman on a cold, January night. But the Lord uses the ordinary things in our lives to put us right where He wants us to be. It is there that He can use us for His glorious purposes.

If you are watching and waiting, and if you are listening for His voice and putting it all into God's hand, there is a good chance you will start seeing God's hand in everything.

12 / A STILL SMALL VOICE
GOD'S GRACE WHISPERS TO US

THE PROPHET ELIJAH was running for his life. Elijah had prayed for a drought that would last three and a half years. And he had made a fool of the king by executing the king's false prophets. He had been part of one of the greatest miracles in the Bible, and he had proven to Israel that God was the only true God.

But this infuriated the king's wife, Jezebel. So, she threatened his life for what he had done. And Elijah ran in fear.

Elijah was a prophet of God, but we learn in James 5 that "Elijah was a man with a nature like ours" (James 5:17 (NKJV)). God spoke to him and used him in mighty ways. Yet, Elijah was not immune to fear or discouragement, and he questioned God's calling at times.

At the end of his running, Elijah found himself alone in a cave, wishing he was dead. He felt like he would be hunted for the rest of his life. God was asking for his obedience. And Elijah didn't understand what God was doing.

We find this story in First Kings 19. The Bible says:

> And there he went into a cave, and spent the night in that place; and behold, the word of the LORD came to him, and He said to him, "What are you doing here, Elijah?" (1 Kings 19:9 (NKJV))

Like so many of us, Elijah was running scared when a difficult situation arose that he didn't think he could handle. Instead of believing in God and doing what he had been asked to do, he found himself leaning on his own understanding. Elijah thought he had to deal with this issue on his own because he didn't understand that God was in control.

But God gave Elijah a lesson. God told him:

> "Go out, and stand on the mountain before the LORD." And behold, the LORD passed by, and a great and strong wind tore into the mountains and broke the rocks in pieces before the LORD, but the LORD was not in the wind; and after the wind an earthquake, but the LORD was not in the earthquake; and after the earthquake a fire, but the LORD was not in the fire; and after the fire a still small voice. (1 Kings 19:11–12 (NKJV))

Elijah had once triumphed in the mountaintop victory at Mount Carmel—a victory given by God Himself. But now, in his new circumstances, he wasn't feeling God's presence in the same way. He had forgotten that God was still in control. This lack of trust consumed Elijah, and he was overtaken by fear.

But the Lord showed him that He could not be found in the monumental and scary events. Instead, God came to Elijah in a "still small voice" (1 Kings 19:12 (NKJV)) . . . a voice that could only be heard when Elijah took the time to slow down and be still.

Now I admit, I was not running for my life. But I was "running" with fear all the same. Although I was hearing God's voice telling me to go and visit a family who lived on my patrol beat, I had to make sure I had my own rules in place. I only wanted to go at certain times when I could avoid uncomfortable situations. I would learn that, for a time, my fear would drown out the still small voice. And when it did, it took me out of God's will.

The family was not the most well-liked family in the cul-de-sac. They had different racial ties than anyone else on the street. And because the younger adults in the household had caused some mayhem in the neighborhood, the neighbors around them didn't like them very much.

Because the family had lost their neighbors' trust, the police were called to their house a lot. There had been numerous police contacts for gang issues, physical fighting, and even gunshots that came from a party at their house. It made the house a target for all kinds of mischief. The house became public enemy number one. I had been there during several intense situations myself, and I never went to the house without several other officers to make our approach as safe as possible.

But the Lord was working in my heart. God was up to something.

Unlike other officers, I knew, behind the disrespectful young adults who caused all the drama, there was an older husband and wife there who knew the Lord. They were a precious couple named Paul and Martha. I had prayed for Martha and for her alcoholism several years before.

In the recent past, I had urged Paul to make peace with his neighbors, so the police would not be the first option for them when anything went wrong. This peacemaking effort is actually Biblical. The Bible instructs us:

> Moreover if your brother sins against you, go and tell him his fault between you and him alone. If he hears you, you have gained your brother. (Matthew 18:15 (NKJV))

I was hoping these truths spoken by Jesus would start mending fences and help restore relations with the neighbors. It has always been my hope that a little diplomacy would reduce the need for correction, especially when I was the correction. In today's day and age, it was a bold suggestion. And I was encouraged when Paul took it to heart. He told me that he would give it a shot. So I prayed there would be open minds and soft hearts.

Several months passed, and I hadn't heard about any calls at the address. I was wondering how things were going in the family. And I was hoping there had been an olive branch that was bearing fruit.

Over the past two weeks, I had heard the voice of the Lord urging me to go see how this elderly couple was doing. But from my recent encounters at the house, I didn't want to go on certain days, knowing the couple would have their children over for dinner. The children were argumentative and disrespectful to me and my coworkers. Like Elijah, I had already made rules in my own mind about how and when I would go to the house.

But then I learned God had other plans.

I was driving by the street where the house was located, and I was once again urged by the Lord to go check on Paul and Martha. I wrestled with the idea until I got to the end of the street I was driving on. Then I decided I had put the meeting off long enough. Obedience to God's calling is the only option. And I felt I had neglected His instructions.

It was Saturday, and their children weren't supposed to be there—Sunday was their family day. So, I turned my police cruiser around and made my way down the street to the cul-de-sac.

To my surprise (and dismay), all the family cars were parked on the street. They were all there a day early. This made me feel like Elijah as he was running into the cave. I was already putting together the reasons I couldn't go there and why it would be a bad idea to go to the house by myself. They had verbally berated me and the other officers who had been there before. Going alone didn't seem wise. I decided I wasn't going to deal with it, and I thought pushing it off to another day would be better. I turned my car around and left.

In the story of Elijah, after he heard the still small voice of the Lord, he relented from his own thoughts and fears and listened to the Lord's instructions. God told Elijah that he wanted him to go back because His work still needed to be done. Although the situation looked one way, it was actually a very different truth Elijah didn't know about. God was truly in control of the entire situation, including Elijah's safety. Elijah just needed to have faith and obey.

I sat at the end of the street, with my car idling. I felt ashamed I had run from the Lord's calling. I sat there, hoping I would receive different instructions from the Lord. But as it has always been with God, He never changes His mind. God is immutable and unchanging.

God told me that I had to go back. His instructions weren't from a booming voice or a loud and obnoxious person walking by. They were in a still small voice. But that voice echoed in my mind, and it ignited my heart. So, I turned my car around once again and went back to the house. I knew the Lord would protect me because He had called me to it.

When I arrived, one of the family members asked me in a stern voice what I wanted. I asked to speak to the husband and wife of the house. To my relief, he went in to get them without a verbal challenge.

Paul and Martha came out, and it was apparent they remembered me. Paul shook my hand and addressed me as "pastor." But since I am a police officer, Martha's first question was, "What did we do now? Who called about us?"

I beamed a smile at her and said, "No one called." I told her that I was there to check up on her and her husband.

But she wasn't buying it and asked again, "Really, who called you?"

I told her it was actually God who called me about them and sent me to check on them. I told her how I had been asked to come by for several weeks, but I had been reluctant when all their family was around.

She told me they had moved the family day to Saturday this week. It was then I knew God wanted me there when they were all around. The conversation continued, and it brought a solemn look to Martha's face.

That's when I knew I had a much deeper reason God had led me to their home. I told her it didn't look like she was doing very well. With tears welling up in her eyes, she nodded her head in agreement.

Paul told me that they had recently received news. After an abnormal medical test, the doctors thought his cancer might have returned. He and his bride of almost thirty years were waiting for the test results. They were discouraged and afraid.

We talked about marriage, faith, and what God was doing through the hardships in their lives. The conversation choked her up, and she went into the house in tears.

Paul told me how he had been in the hospital for six months with cancer. His immune system had been so weak he couldn't have visitors. He told me, in the "prison cell" of his hospital bed, he prayed a lot and was forced to lean on the Lord for comfort. He was confident, if this was the same outcome, he would be content with whatever the Lord had planned. His wife was not so optimistic.

I then received a call for service elsewhere, and I was forced to leave. I laid hands on the husband and prayed for healing before I left. But as I was driving to my next destination, the Lord put it on my heart that I had not said or done everything He wanted.

I went back to the house an hour later to read Scripture, pray for Paul *and* his wife together, and anoint them with oil. This is the passage the Lord provided for me to read:

> Is anyone among you suffering? Let him pray. Is anyone cheerful? Let him sing psalms. Is anyone among you sick? Let him call for the elders of the church, and let them pray

over him, anointing him with oil in the name of the Lord. And the prayer of faith will save the sick, and the Lord will raise him up. And if he has committed sins, he will be forgiven. Confess your trespasses to one another, and pray for one another, that you may be healed. The effective, fervent prayer of a righteous man avails much. Elijah was a man with a nature like ours, and he prayed earnestly that it would not rain; and it did not rain on the land for three years and six months. And he prayed again, and the heaven gave rain, and the earth produced its fruit. (James 5:13–18 (NKJV))

I learned during the next conversation that Martha had slipped into a great depression and had been drinking heavily—a problem I had prayed about several years before. I anointed them both with oil and said a prayer that must have come from the Spirit of God Himself.

When I said amen, I looked at Paul and said, "Now, I have said all I need to say." And I gave him the prayer stone I had in my pocket.

I often carried these resin stones as part of my ministry. When I meet someone who needs encouragement, I give them a stone. Apparently, this particular stone was for him. The Lord had purposed it for Paul when I had prayed over it earlier in the month. Martha thanked me for being bold and stepping out to care for them, to love and serve them.

I hoped the young people in the house asked for an explanation of why I was there. And I hoped the couple told them what happened. My prayer for the house went along the same lines as a verse in the Book of Matthew:

> Let your light so shine before men, that they may see your
> good works and glorify your Father in heaven.
> (Matthew 5:16 (NKJV))

How beautiful it would be if the Lord called for a revival in their house and brought healing and restoration to their parents. How awesome it would be if the Lord would be glorified in such a place. How amazing it would be if they came to an understanding of God's grace and mercy through the most unlikely of people . . . a police officer.

Paul called me a few days later to tell me that the tests had come back negative. He had a clean bill of health. I met up with him a few days later and gave him a hug. We rejoiced in the wonderful work of God.

But this didn't end our relationship . . . hard times would come again.

Many are the storms of a tormented man. I learned a few months later that Martha had started abusing alcohol again. The emotional toil had led to them getting divorced.

I sat in that living room with Paul and some of those young adults I had been afraid of for so long—just talking as if we were friends. I found Martha in her new apartment, and I prayed with her and her daughter as well. They were so thankful for a kind and supportive voice.

And then I learned that you never know whom you touch, even months later.

About six months later, I received a call from a former sergeant of mine while I was at home, recovering from surgery. He told me that Paul had passed away. The family had told him that "a bald officer" had been at the house numerous times to care for and pray with him. He instantly knew it was me—the bald officer who prays. His hunch was confirmed when he saw numerous calls for service at the address, initiated by me. The notes had nothing criminal and nothing spectacular; they simply read "checked up on residents."

You never know the impact you might have when you follow the Lord's leading. Insert yourself into someone's life and see what the Lord will do with it.

Which brings me to one more thing. As we saw in the above passage in James, "Elijah was a man with a nature like ours" (James 5:17 (NKJV)). This means God uses and hears the prayers of simple people, flawed people, and scared people, just like us. So, you're not off the hook just because you're not a pastor.

We won't always know what God is planning when we hear His still small voice. But His desire is for us to take the next step. We must be obedient to what He asks whether we understand it or not.

In the Book of Psalms, King David tells us this truth plainly:

> Your word is a lamp to my feet and a light to my path.
> (Psalm 119:105 (NKJV))

God's instructions aren't a beacon, illuminating far into your future. There is only light to guide your next few steps.

I had no idea what God had planned when He tasked me with going to talk with this couple. As it turned out, the Lord used me to minister to and serve a family full of His precious people who were in desperate need of encouragement.

As Jeremiah wrote:

O Lord, I know the way of man is not in himself; it is not in man who walks to direct his own steps. (Jeremiah 10:23 (NKJV))

Trust in the Lord. If He calls you to do something, be obedient to do it. As the second part of this verse points out, if you are a man or a woman who walks the walk of faith in the Lord, then you won't have to direct your own steps. In God's infinite wisdom, His steps are far better than yours.

So, stand up. Listen. Take action. And see that the Lord is truly good!

13 / THE RIFLEMAN

GOD'S GRACE COVERS AND PROTECTS US

I RACKED the charging handle hard on my patrol rifle. It's calls like these that are the most intense because you know there's a higher chance that someone is going to get hurt or even killed. Dispatch advised that a male had pointed a gun at his girlfriend. She was locked in the bedroom and couldn't get out of the house.

We respond to calls involving guns all the time. It's our desire to have better weapons and equipment than the other guy, so we can do our job more safely and effectively. That's why I was carrying my patrol rifle. It's more powerful and more accurate than what he had . . . or at least that's what I was hoping.

I took up a position at the side of the house, laying down in the grass for safety. My sights were trained on the back door of the small condo. If I saw him come outside with a gun, I would be in a position to see him before he saw me. This would give me the advantage and time to handle whatever threat he might bring.

But I swallowed hard when dispatch came across the radio again to give us more information. The male inside was a former Marine. He was intoxicated and a weapons fanatic. His girlfriend, who was still hiding in the master bedroom, told us that he had threatened her with an FN FAL rifle, which used .308 rounds. That's a bullet our protective equipment cannot stop.

In a moment, we went from having better guns and equipment to being behind the curve. That, along with the facts that he had combat training and experience and was emotionally unstable, quickly evolved it into a very dangerous situation.

I didn't have any cover. If I moved to the tree, which was adequate to stop his bullet, I would not be able to see the back door. Without coverage of the back door, he would have an unseen escape route. Or, worse yet, he would be able to ambush the officers in the front of the house. I laid as flat as I could and peered down the end of my rifle sights. I was going to have to be fast and accurate to beat his superior weaponry.

In times like these, we can do two things. We can retreat, or we can stay. Retreating would ensure our safety. But there is no valor in running. I became a police officer to run toward these types of situations. And besides, we weren't the only ones in danger. We needed to get the woman out of the house.

It was at that point I visited one of my trusty habits: I prayed.

Praying is just another way of saying, "I talked to God." I have a close relationship with God because He has adopted me as His son. As Paul told the Ephesians:

> All praise to God, the Father of our Lord Jesus Christ, who has blessed us with every spiritual blessing in the heavenly realms because we are united with Christ. Even before He made the world, God loved us and chose us in Christ to be

holy and without fault in His eyes. God decided in advance to adopt us into His own family by bringing us to Himself through Jesus Christ. This is what He wanted to do, and it gave Him great pleasure. So we praise God for the glorious grace He has poured out on us who belong to His dear Son. (Ephesians 1:3–6 (NLT))

The Scriptures are full of verses that tell us God loves His children. And when we talk to Him, He delights in us. When we ask Him things, He hears us and answers us. When we ask for things in His name and along the tracks of His will for our lives, it becomes clear that we can see His faithfulness when things happen around us (*see, e.g.*, John 14:13).

I took this assurance into prayer. As I lay in the open greenbelt, I prayed for the outcome of a tense situation. I asked:

God, Please deliver this man into our hands without violence. I ask that no one would be hurt and that he would come to his senses and give up without an incident. In Your providence, Lord, you can make people do things they have no intention of doing. You can change the minds and hearts of even those people who don't believe in You. And You can make things happen so Your will is done to Your glory. In this, Lord, please protect us and show your faithfulness to those whom you have ordained to handle these evil situations, as it tells us in Romans 13:1–4. In Jesus' name, amen.

We were able to get the young lady out of a window. Now we had a man with heavy artillery in a house by himself. Those are the times when things can get really ugly. When a man knows he is surrounded and things are not going his way, he can become desperate. We were trying to be ready for anything.

The lieutenant on the scene called him twice, but his cell phone went straight to voicemail. He left a message, and we were left to make a new plan. (The lieutenant later told me that he never actually talked to the man while we were there.)

I prayed again that God would deliver this man into our hands without violence, and that He would change his heart and mind to give up on this path he was walking down.

I thought about a story I had just recently read in the Bible where God stirred up the heart of an unbelieving king named Cyrus to deliver the Israelites from Babylonian captivity (2 Chronicles 36:22–23). In one of the most powerful prophesies in the Bible, the Prophet Isaiah said this of King Cyrus:

> Thus says the LORD to His anointed, to Cyrus, whose right hand I have held—to subdue nations before him and loose the armor of kings, to open before him the double doors, so that the gates will not be shut:

> "I will go before you and make the crooked places straight; I will break in pieces the gates of bronze and cut the bars of iron. I will give you the treasures of darkness and hidden riches of secret places, that you may know that I, the LORD, Who call you by your name, am the God of Israel." (Isaiah 45:1–3 (NKJV))

I thought about the sovereignty of God and how God can change the heart of anyone (like that of King Cyrus) so He can fulfill His plans and purposes. This call was going to need that kind of work from God. These are the calls that lead us to call in SWAT and our hostage negotiators. These calls take a long time. And they often don't end well.

But then something interesting happened. As I was praying, the male walked out of the front door with his hands up. He was calmly taken into custody without incident and got into the back of a waiting patrol car. It certainly looked like God might have answered my prayer for surrender. But what I would learn shortly afterward made the Lord answering my prayer a complete certainty.

As our officers walked through the house after his arrest, it became clear he was not initially ready to surrender. We found military-grade weapons in every room. He had stowed ballistic body armor and ammunition in the crawl space in case we entered the house. It looked like the gun fanatic was ready for war against us. And he had the firepower to do it.

But it became evident that God was on our side. Officers found an AR-15 pattern rifle on the floor, under a blanket, next to the couch in the front room. The window shades were down just enough for him to see the entire cul-de-sac without allowing us to see inside. He had multiple magazines full of rounds.

If he had wanted to, he could have easily killed any one of the officers who were taking cover behind buildings and cars just yards away from his living room window. It certainly appeared he had taken a sniper position and had put his rifle sights on cops before changing his mind. Thank the Lord this man didn't decide to fire.

A similar story happened in the Bible too. In the Book of First Samuel, we find King Saul continuing his pursuit of David, God's newly anointed king. Saul was jealous and paranoid of David, and he wanted him dead. He had spent years trying to catch the fleeing David in the wilderness.

> When Saul and his men went to seek him, they told David. Therefore he went down to the rock, and stayed in the Wilderness of Maon. And when Saul heard that, he pursued David in the Wilderness of Maon. Then Saul went on one side of the mountain, and David and his men on the other side of the mountain. So David made haste to get away from Saul, for Saul and his men were encircling David and his men to take them.
>
> But a messenger came to Saul, saying, "Hurry and come, for the Philistines have invaded the land!" Therefore Saul returned from pursuing David, and went against the Philistines; so they called that place the Rock of Escape. (1 Samuel 23:25–28 (NKJV))

David and his men were in grave danger. They were being pursued by a vengeful man and were greatly outnumbered by a large army. And they were facing an attack from all sides. It was a tense time for David.

But just like our situation with this gunman in his home, God was making things happen. God stirred up the ungodly people known as the Philistines to attack the Israelites, which caused Saul to have to withdraw from his pursuit of David to protect his city and his people.

Similarly, God's sovereignty changed this man's heart, and he calmly surrendered. It was a direct answer to my prayer for God to deliver the man into our hands without violence. We all took a collective sigh of relief. I stowed my rifle, and I headed off to the hospital to talk to the man's girlfriend.

In hindsight, this was where I saw God's hand move again. I wasn't the one who was supposed to go and talk to her. It wasn't my investigation, and it wasn't my patrol area. I had no business doing anything else during this call. But because God's hand was moving—because He was preemptively shaping the narrative for something that would actually happen the next day—He wanted me to build a relationship with this man's girlfriend, the victim in this case.

It's important to know that God is always working. He is moving mountains around, just outside your vision. So when the pieces all fall together, it looks like it was meant to be that way all along.

That's what I saw in this case too. The time I had at the hospital was not really that big a deal. There wasn't anything spiritual about it. I just gave time and information to a young lady who had gone through a really scary situation. But the next day, I would liken this hostage incident to the explosive power of a bomb.

The military uses an explosive called C4. It's a very effective explosive because it brings a great deal of damaging force and power. But without an ignition charge, it's harmless. You can throw it around, toss it in your bag, or even light it on fire and it won't explode. It is very stable. But if you add a blasting cap, which is itself a small explosive, it creates enough energy to make the C4 explode. It's a powerful chain reaction that allows the chemical detonation to take place.

This was the image the Lord had given me as I was driving to the girlfriend's house the next afternoon. It didn't make much sense to me right away. But He made it clearer as I got closer to my destination. As God had set it up, the filing detective in the case needed me to have the young lady sign a consent form so we could move on with the case against the gunman. God had been moving mountains.

After I completed the administrative stuff I had been sent there to do by the detective, I started to tell the young lady this story from my standpoint. I told her how God had orchestrated all of this in her life to illustrate a point. It was then that the C4 analogy made sense—an analogy given by God to a "military brat," born into a military family, who would easily understand what it meant.

As scary as the ordeal was for her, it only represented the blasting cap. God used an explosive situation to initiate a greater, more powerful explosive situation—the sharing of the gospel of Jesus Christ.

I have found as I share my faith that, in and of itself, the gospel usually doesn't bring a very powerful reaction in people . . . until something out of the ordinary happens to open their eyes to their vulnerabilities. This circumstance was no different.

I got the sense that she was not a believer in God just by the way she reacted to my story. But when I told her that God's grace and love had allowed her to survive the incident, and that God gave her another day to consider her decision between Jesus and the world, between heaven and hell, tears ran down her cheeks.

God had allowed her to get to the hospital. And He had allowed me to be the one to build a relationship with her there. God had brought me to her house under the need to have a form signed and had given me the discernment and boldness to profess His love for her. That is *explosive*!

God answers your prayers. He wants to have a relationship with you so badly. And He wants to use you in mighty ways.

As Peter said:

All praise to God, the Father of our Lord Jesus Christ. It is by His great mercy that we have been born again, because God raised Jesus Christ from the dead. Now we live with great expectation, and we have a priceless inheritance—an inheritance that is kept in heaven for you, pure and undefiled, beyond the reach of change and decay. And through your faith, God is protecting you by His power until you receive this salvation, which is ready to be revealed on the last day for all to see. (1 Peter 1:3–5 (NLT))

The Lord of heaven protected us in our dealings with this incident. He caused an otherwise violent man to surrender on his own, delivering him into our hands without violence. He protected the young lady and allowed her to get out of the house safely. He had allowed an injury to her knee from jumping out of a window, so she would have to get medical attention.

He sent me, out of my area, to the hospital to build a relationship. He sent me again, to her house the next day, by the order of an unrelated person. And He guided in me the will and courage to preach the gospel. He even gave me an analogy that would be understood by this precious, military family.

God truly does work all things together for the good of those who love Him (Romans 8:28). Praise Him!

14 / TREASURE IN THE FIELD

GOD'S GRACE FINDS US WHEN WE'RE LOST

"Do you want to be made well?"

As a police officer, I found myself dealing with people who could not decide the answer to this question. And lately, it had been a greater and greater truth in my walk.

The tear stains on my uniform showed me all too often the hurt and brokenness people were feeling. And this was a powerful question I asked more often than I used to. Maybe it was a growing spiritual maturity. Or maybe it was Jesus moving through me to get to the heart of the matter.

In the Bible, we find that Jesus posed this very question to a paralyzed man lying near the Pool of Bethesda. I don't think there is much doubt that, at this point in Jesus' ministry, this man knew who Jesus was. He had probably heard about the miracles of healing Jesus had been doing in the city and around the region. And when Jesus approached him on a personal level, choosing him over all the other sick people there, you would believe you could predict how he would have answered that question.

But to the surprise of many, the man's answer seemed a bit off base. So, let's see what happened.

> When Jesus saw him lying there, and knew that he already had been in that condition a long time, He said to him, "Do you want to be made well?"
>
> The sick man answered Him, "Sir, I have no man to put me into the pool when the water is stirred up; but while I am coming, another steps down before me." (John 5:6–7 (NKJV))

The King of healing was standing before this man, a man who had been paralyzed for thirty-eight years. And Jesus asked him a very direct and pointed question. Yet, instead of answering His question in faith, the man made excuses.

In our culture, there are more than a few ways to seek healing. Everywhere you turn, there are liquor stores and dispensaries; pharmacies and psychiatrists; hospitals and self-help books that send people clamoring for the latest and greatest way to get away from whatever ails them in this life.

At the pool of Bethesda, it was no different: healing to the one who got in the water first. I can imagine the scene—people with all kinds of issues—clamoring to get to the water. And I can imagine the discouragement of those who had just missed out or who couldn't get to the water in the first place.

This reminds me of Jennifer, a young woman I've come into contact with on a number of occasions. I have asked her several times if she wanted to be made well from her severe alcoholism. Her answer has always been an excuse.

Just as this man was approached by Jesus Himself, I can tell you that Jesus has approached her as well. And there is no incident more miraculous than His life-saving hands on her one day in late October.

On that day, Jennifer had consumed a tremendous amount of alcohol. While she was intoxicated, she left her mother's house. She had been homeless most of the summer because, when she drinks, she gets violent. Her mother, who cares for young children, could not allow her around the house for their safety. So when Jennifer drinks, she must go.

On several occasions, I have sat with Jennifer in the hospital, praying for her and sharing the gospel. The last time I talked to her, several months before, I had read her the following Scripture:

> The Spirit of the LORD is upon Me, because He has anointed Me to preach the gospel to the poor; He has sent Me to heal the brokenhearted, to proclaim liberty to the captives and recovery of sight to the blind, to set at liberty those who are oppressed; to proclaim the acceptable year of the LORD. (Luke 4:18–19 (NKJV))

Jennifer was confident she fit all the categories of people whom Jesus said He was sent to save. I told her healing was in the name of Jesus Christ. But she still offered excuses.

On that day in October, she got her stuff together and left the house. Her mother told me later that evening she and her oldest son had gone out to look for her. But they were unable to find her. It was a pleasant fall day. However, with a forecast of adverse weather later in the evening, she was worried.

We couldn't see it at the time, but God was working.

In another part of the city, a man was getting ready for work. He let his two dogs out into the backyard to get some exercise. And his small dog escaped the confines of his backyard into the greenbelt behind his house. The man went back and trounced through the high grass and brush looking for his dog. He quickly found him and went home. Then he went to work as normal.

The term *God's providence* can best be defined as: "The governance of God by which He, with wisdom and love, cares for and directs all things in the universe."[1]

I have talked a number of times about God's providence—the beautiful truth that God has sovereign control over absolutely everything. God moves people and places and actions around to make things happen, to bring people into contact with Himself.

Could it be that the dog getting out early in the morning was God's way of setting up a series of decisions by the man later in the evening? Would God use the circumstances for His glory and magnificence?

When the man got home from work, he again let his dogs out into the backyard. And when he heard his largest dog scratching at the back door, he went to let his dogs inside. When he got there, he found that, once again, his smaller dog was missing.

Immediately, the man knew how the dog had escaped and where to find him. He put on his jacket because it was near dusk and the temperature was quickly dropping. Then he went out to save his little dog.

The man was again walking through the brush, calling for his lost dog. The scrub brush back there was five to six feet high in places, and it was hard to find the little dog in the area. He continued calling his dog as he stepped through a large collection of tumbleweeds and brush. In the brush, he found a woman tucked back inside an area that had been cleared out. It seemed she was dead because his continuous calling to her provided zero response. He called 911.

I was the first one on the scene. And when the man led me into the weeds where the woman was lying, she was alive. She was breathing but in a full-on seizure. I recognized her; it was Jennifer. When she came out of her seizure, I assisted her to an ambulance.

As the ambulance pulled away, I examined the scene to make sure nothing criminal had happened to her. I determined there was absolutely no way to see her from the path, and there was no way for a passing car to see or hear her.

She was wearing a t-shirt and thin pants. She didn't have any other clothing with her and wasn't dressed for the pending temperature drop. If she had remained there in that state, she most likely would have died of hypothermia and the seizures brought on by her intoxication. God had once again, and in a miraculous way, saved Jennifer's life.

What's more, I had been out sick for the two prior shifts. Although I wasn't feeling any better, I felt compelled to go to work, as if the hand of God was on me to go. Because I was at work, God sent me—His servant—to be the first person she saw when she came out of her seizure.

Remember the definition of providence I provided earlier? "The governance of God by which He, with wisdom and love, cares for and directs all things in the universe."

With wisdom and *love*, He *cares* for us. God had saved her life *again* and sent me to share the gospel *again*, in *love*. God could have used anyone. Had I called in sick, it would have been just that, another officer. But obedience to my Lord is paramount in my walk. Faithfulness to His calling is all I care about in this life. I *love* because *He* first loved me (1 John 4:19).

The first trip to the hospital that night didn't gain much traction. She was really out of it. But I laid my hand on her forehead and prayed for her. I could tell she knew I had prayed because she smiled through the oxygen mask and fought to sit up to give me a hug.

Man, seeing anyone in that condition is heart-wrenching. But it's especially heart-wrenching when you have dealt with them multiple times and have even asked the question, "Do you want to be made well?"

The second time, which was about two hours later, was much better. I remember arguing with God that driving all the way back to the hospital was a strange request. I wondered what good it could do—Jennifer was in really bad shape and me trying to talk to her in that condition wasn't going to do much. But God's order on my heart got more intense, and I kept driving toward the emergency room. The Lord has a funny way of requesting things that don't seem to make sense.

When I got back into the room, Jennifer was completely coherent. I was able to talk to her again for about thirty minutes. Can you guess what I asked her? Yep . . .

Do you want to be made well?

I learned over that half-hour that she had recently attended the substance abuse program at my church, although she had quit.

She told me she had accepted Christ as her Savior. That was news to me, and I thanked the Lord. My whole reason for being there this time was to make sure she had accepted Jesus as her Savior—that she had been "born again"—before we found her dead somewhere.

I was happy about that. I continued to share with her that there were others besides me who were worried about her and who had been praying for her. I prayed for her again and left the hospital.

I learned something about Jennifer during all of this: the available excuses at her disposal were dwindling. God was working in her life. God continued to send eager, Jesus-loving people to help her. God loves her enough to be patient and to create miracles in an effort to keep her alive, even after her foolish and self-destructive choices.

Does she want to be made well? I think she does. Will I ever see her made well? Only God knows. But the Word tells us that Jesus is the way.

As we finish the passage about the man at the Pool of Bethesda, we see that, despite his excuses for why he couldn't be healed, our Lord Jesus healed him anyway.

> Jesus said to him, "Rise, take up your bed and walk." And immediately the man was made well, took up his bed, and walked.
>
> And that day was the Sabbath. (John 5:8–9 (NKJV))

For Jennifer, and many others God has pinned on my heart to pray for, I proclaim that healing is in Jesus. Freedom is in Jesus. Clarity and sobriety come from Jesus. And I will not stop telling her (and others) this very fact until the day I stand before Him myself, completely healed.

Do you know something? God is amazingly patient with us. I learned this truth as I drove my patrol car around in my daily routine. He is patient, both for me and for those I worked around. He knows our weaknesses. He knows our shortcomings. But He also knows our propensity to love others in the name of His Son. And He knows that heaven awaits those who choose wisely.

The Bible promises us:

> But, beloved, do not forget this one thing, that with the Lord one day is as a thousand years, and a thousand years as one day. The Lord is not slack concerning His promise, as some count slackness, but is longsuffering toward us, not willing that any should perish but that all should come to repentance. (2 Peter 3:8–9 (NKJV))

Miracles happen every day. My prayer for you is that you would hear God's voice and act accordingly—that you would ask others if they want to be made well and introduce them to Jesus, the Healer. I pray you will keep your spiritual eyes open, following Jesus with the faith of a child.

No one is out of His reach. And the acts of love you take to others will never get past the Lord. And who knows . . . you might just see a miracle.

15 / LOCK PICKS

GOD'S GRACE GIVES US TALENTS
TO SHARE WITH OTHERS

DURING THE PANDEMIC, they said police officers were "essential personnel." I suppose that goes without saying. Even on a normal day, we are still considered essential.

I'm not completely sure society would know what to do if we weren't around. So as I pinned on my badge and strapped on my service weapon, I had to remember, for better or for worse —whether I wanted to be or not—I was needed out there.

But what if there were deeper needs that we as essential personnel needed to fill? And what if those needs weren't police issues but spiritual ones? In that perspective, *all* Christians should be considered "essential personnel."

One of my favorite tools I used on duty was my lock picks. I taught myself the technique of picking locks as a way to pass the time. But I never knew God would use it in so many different ways during my police career.

I have used lock picks to get

- families back into their houses when they accidentally lock themselves out;

- the fire department into locations to fix water leaks when no one was home;
- detectives into the houses of suspects to serve search warrants without damaging the front door;
- entry to recover the remains of those who had died alone; and
- entry into the homes of concerned loved ones and, in doing so, have brought a sigh of relief when those houses were found to be empty.

I can safely say that this skill has allowed me to serve my community well. But it was God who gave me the skill. The Bible says:

> Blessed be the LORD my Rock, who trains my hands for war, and my fingers for battle. (Psalm 144:1 (NKJV))

I've learned that God's gifts and talents don't discount our need for continued training and experience. We need to put emphasis on the work we do to perfect our talents.

Personally, I believe striving to be at our best as we perfect our God-given abilities is how we worship the Lord. It's our chance to give an emphatic "thank you" for the gifts He has so graciously given us. Some people are great singers, some are tremendous writers or speakers, some are amazing evangelists, and some can pick locks from time to time.

In the parable of the talents (Matthew 25:14–30), Jesus told His disciples about a rich man (lord) who gave "talents" to three of his servants. At the time, a talent was a measure of money. But this parable also works for our understanding of our gifts and talents; the stuff we do very well. The rich man returned to judge those servants on how they used those talents while he was gone.

The Bible says:

> After a long time the lord of those servants came and settled accounts with them.
>
> So he who had received five talents came and brought five other talents, saying, "Lord, you delivered to me five talents; look, I have gained five more talents besides them." His lord said to him, "Well done, good and faithful servant; you were faithful over a few things, I will make you ruler over many things. Enter into the joy of your lord." (Matthew 25:19–21 (NKJV))

This parable expresses the joy set by God (the rich man) for those who work with, invest, and improve their talents for the kingdom of God.

As the parable continues, the man likewise, who had given two talents to a second servant, gave him the same praise. He said, "Well done, good and faithful servant; you were faithful over a few things, I will make you ruler over many things" (Matthew 25:23 (NKJV)). His response shows it isn't how many talents you have but how you use and improve them for God's kingdom.

But there was also a third servant in the parable—one who took his single talent and buried it in the ground. In essence, he didn't use, improve, or invest his talent at all. This led to a sharp rebuke from the rich man. The rich man told him that he was wicked, lazy, and had not been a good steward of what he had been given.

The rebuke was daunting, to say the least:

> For to everyone who has, more will be given, and he will have abundance; but from him who does not have, even what he has will be taken away. And cast the unprofitable servant into the outer darkness. There will be weeping and gnashing of teeth. (Matthew 25:29–30 (NKJV))

This last passage reminds me of the verse in Luke that says, "[T]o whom much is given, from him much will be required" (Luke 12:48 (NKJV)). In essence, how you use the talents you are given is directly tied to your rewards, both here on the earth and in heaven. And that's a pretty big charge!

Before he even became king, David knew the relationship between his talents and abilities and God's laser-focused will to use those skills for His glory. As David told Saul:

> "Your servant used to keep his father's sheep, and when a lion or a bear came and took a lamb out of the flock, I went out after it and struck it, and delivered the lamb from its mouth; and when it arose against me, I caught it by its beard, and struck and killed it. Your servant has killed both lion and bear; and this uncircumcised Philistine will be like one of them, seeing he has defied the armies of the living God." Moreover David said, "The LORD, who delivered me from the paw of the lion and from the paw of the bear, He will deliver me from the hand of this Philistine." (1 Samuel 17:34–37 (NKJV))

We are told that David became an expert marksman with his sling and a stone. He had trained and practiced his trade. This allowed him to be a successful shepherd—one who could protect his herd from the bear and the lion.

But David also understood the Lord had a significant part to play in his abilities. He proclaimed it was God who would deliver him from Goliath, not himself and his skills. David understood the balance between the thousands of stones he had slung in practice, his "God-given" talent to hit his target, and God's providence that allowed his stone to find its mark— even to bring down the giant.

Understanding this balance is important. I want to illustrate this further in a lesson I learned over two calls for service in the same shift.

God gave me the talent of picking locks, and I try to practice the art as much as I can. I have a healthy understanding that it is His providence that allows me to glorify Him in this manner. And I have learned this simple truth: if the Lord wants me in the house, and I do the mechanical work of manipulating the lock, then He will lead my hands to line up the pins and allow the tumblers to move. But when the Lord doesn't want me inside the house, it doesn't matter how easy or complex the lock is or how long I work on it, it won't unlock.

This is a story about two such locks.

At the beginning of my shift, I was sent to attempt contact with a woman who had not been heard from for a few weeks. After the government's call to stay home and self-quarantine due to the global COVID-19 pandemic, she left work, and no one had talked to her. They told me that she had some mental issues and had been depressed.

I knocked on the door but didn't get an answer. There were two cars in the driveway. I went around to the backyard to try to see inside the house through a window. I pushed open the back door, which was unlocked.

It became apparent that the woman who lived there had some hoarding behaviors. There was so much stuff in the house I could not push the door open more than a few inches. I made a verbal announcement but got no answer. And then I was hit in the face by the rancid odor of decay. My heart sank.

I walked around to the front door. I needed to see if I could get into the house to recover what I expected to be her body. The doorknob was broken, and the deadbolt lock was damaged. I used my lock picks hoping the Lord would allow me into the house. The tumbler moved quickly, and the lock was defeated. I pushed the damaged door open. I was again smacked by the stench a lot of officers have taken in when we seek to recover those loved ones who have passed away.

I made another loud, verbal announcement as I prepared to press into the house. And then my sinking heart was met with an uplifting sound . . . a little voice from the back room.

As it turned out, the woman was alive and okay. The smell I had taken in a few minutes earlier turned out to be rotting food and garbage in the house—an observation that is normal and prominent among those who suffer from hoarding behaviors.

Relieved she was actually alive, I talked to the elderly woman for a long while. In this new, impersonal policing world wrought with the definitions of social distancing and personal quarantine, it had been hard for me to feel I was making a difference—that I was serving the citizens with the love of Christ.

I learned she was alone and cut off from any social interaction because she didn't have any family or friends. Her only interpersonal contact had been with coworkers at her job. Unfortunately, due to the restrictions from the COVID-19 virus, her job had been closed. She didn't have the technology to stay in touch, and she felt very isolated.

She had suffered from depression for most of her seventy-plus years, and things were getting harder and harder every day. I could hear the distance in her voice. And then I realized something: what I initially thought was the recovery of a dead body was, instead, the opportunity to recover a lost soul.

I told her that she wasn't alone. And I took the opportunity to introduce her to Jesus. I was able to tell her all about what Jesus had done for her on the cross. I told her that the "hell" she lived in was not worthy to be compared to heaven, and God wanted to be the loving Father she never had. It was probably the most complete Biblical encouragement I have ever had the opportunity to share with someone who was an unbeliever. I prayed with her before leaving the house.

I don't know what the Holy Spirit will do in her life. The Bible says there is no pressure on me to "sell" her into being a believer in Jesus Christ. We can plant or water seeds of God's love into someone's life like a farmer does his crops. We can cultivate and turn up the ground. And we can give the seeds nutrients and sun. But the real miracle that allows the seed to grow is done by God alone.

I guess it is still to be seen if the Spirit will remove the little stone in her heart and replace it with flesh and the love of Christ. What I can tell you is this—in God's eyes, I was essential personnel. He had developed the skills I needed to complete the mission He deployed me to. Yes, it's true my badge put me in the right place to share the gospel with a hurting and lonely heart.

But Jesus told us:

> [Y]ou shall receive power when the Holy Spirit has come upon you; and you shall be witnesses to Me in Jerusalem, and in all Judea and Samaria, and to the end of the earth. (Acts 1:8 (NKJV))

There is nothing stopping you from becoming essential personnel by taking the love of Christ and the gospel to a neighborhood, city, state, country, and even a world that is hurting like this woman. God *is* love, and anything you do in love is tangible evidence of His existence. In these times, there is more than enough fear, pain, anxiety, and isolation to go around. In God's eyes, we are "essential" in His will.

The woman was thankful I was able to get her doorknob unlocked so she could replace it. She was also happy to have someone to talk to—a stranger who showed care and concern for her. She was a woman who, in her heart, felt unworthy of love. But showing God's love to her was the cure.

The next day I repaired her door so she could lock up her house. She asked me why I took the time to do what I did for her. I told her the love of Christ compelled me to do it. God was glorified because I took my essential personnel status in God's army seriously.

God used my hands to unlock the barrier to what might be a *hope* the woman had never felt before in her life. It's the hope that is only found in Jesus Christ. Jesus is our living hope. It reminds me of Ezekiel's conversation with God: "And He said to me, 'Son of man, can these bones live?' So I answered, 'Oh Lord GOD, You know'" (Ezekiel 37:3 (NKJV)).

I hope the love of Jesus will reach her heart before it's too late. I was happy to see, because she was alive, there was a chance God might reach her. Refreshed by the opportunity to serve a needy heart in the love of Christ, I thanked the Lord for the opportunity and went to the next call.

Across town, the Lord had set up the other half of this spiritual lesson. Another officer needed lock picks and, feeling the hot hand, I pointed my car in that direction. When I arrived, I learned the officers on the scene had secured the front door after an investigation but had accidentally left a personal item inside the locked apartment. The Lord and I got to work to recover the backpack behind the locked front door.

I thanked God, and I asked Him to guide my hands to the right place to turn the tumbler of the lock. If He wanted me to gain access to the apartment, His grace would allow me success. It took some time and some patience, but the Lord was gracious again. I pushed the unlocked door open.

Inside, just a few feet from the front door, was the evidence of one who had lost all hope. I didn't have to investigate the gunshot suicide. But the blood pool on the hardwood floor was evidence enough that hope for one man had evaporated.

The coroner retrieved her forgotten bag, and we closed up the apartment. Had there been "essential personnel" in his life to feed him the powerful news I had given to the woman only an hour earlier? I don't know. The badge that had allowed me to bring hope to someone in need was the same badge that showed me there are others who aren't getting it in a timely manner.

I thanked God for the opportunity to serve the young lady who needed to get her backpack. But I sat and meditated on the different facets of these two "picks." Again, God used my hands to unlock the barrier. But this time, the outcome was different.

The lesson was this: one lock pick was met with hope . . . the other one was met with hopelessness. The only difference between the two calls was time. And if the current environment continues to degrade, there is going to be a whole lot more hopelessness and isolation in people. We have a job to do. And I'm not sure how much time we have to do it.

Are you starting to see what "essential personnel" really means? God has called *you* to be essential on His work staff. Your position as a police officer is essential. Your position as a mail carrier or an Amazon driver is essential. Your position as a grocery store or drugstore employee is essential. Your position as a first responder, nurse, doctor, or surgeon is essential.

Are you answering phones from home or a call center? Yep, you are essential. How about making food for someone to pick up? You have been deemed essential. Even your position as a stay-at-home mom who is changing diapers and home-schooling your kids is *essential*. You never know when the gifts and talents God has given you will be called into use by the Creator of the universe to have the biggest effect on someone who is hopeless.

Even when the church's doors are closed, the Church is deployed. The Lord knows everything that's going to happen and when His Church will be needed. Nothing takes Him by surprise. He will use difficult times for your spiritual maturity and His glory. No matter what happens, His standing order hasn't changed.

As Jesus told us:

All authority has been given to Me in heaven and on earth. Go therefore and make disciples of all the nations, baptizing them in the name of the Father and of the Son and of the Holy Spirit, teaching them to observe all things that I have commanded you; and lo, I am with you always, even to the end of the age. (Matthew 28:18–20 (NKJV))

Jesus has called you to "essential personnel" status. So strap on your spiritual armor, practice your skills and talents, and take the love of God to this hurting and hopeless world. For some people you meet, you might be the only hope they have before it's too late. Consider this your deployment orders.

MY HEART WAS heavy as I watched the medical staff feverishly trying to save a man's life. He had just been out on a date . . . out to dinner. How could he have known that his date's jealous ex-husband would be so wicked?

Seven shots, point blank, through the driver-side window. I was in the trauma room of the hospital. I was there to keep an eye on him, update investigators at the scene . . . and provide a time of death for the official report.

I can tell you: I understand what it means when the Bible says the face of Jesus was "so disfigured He seemed hardly human, and from His appearance, one would scarcely know He was a man" (Isaiah 52:14 (NLT)). I was trying to compare the man's face to his driver's license photo. There was no way to compare them, let alone, identify him.

Man, this job is hard!

Homicide called me. They wanted an update. But the time of death never came. I have no idea how he survived the catastrophic injuries he sustained in one hateful and determined course of action by a coward. I continued to stand by, watching the chaos—praying over and over again for this man.

My heart felt like a rock. Pint after pint of blood was put back into his body. Surprisingly, the CAT scan showed no injuries to his brain. Although most of the bones in his face had been shattered, none of them were injuries that would be life threatening. When the doctors were able to get the massive bleeding under control, his situation was just a little more favorable. By God's loving grace, it appeared this man might survive what appeared, at first, to be impossible.

This wasn't the first time I had been in this position. For sixteen years as a police officer in this city, I had watched nightmares happen to other people.

In past years, watching over this man would have been just another call. But a few years before, God had done a work in me so miraculous that, if you knew me before "the change," you would not have believed it. For the first twelve years of police life, the stuff I watched left me with a hard and calloused heart.

Yet, looking back, it wasn't ever one, fist-sized, solid rock. Instead, the soft and tender heart that wanted to help people was slowly being choked out by the small pebbles that had come with call after call of the death, destruction, and hatred a police officer deals with every day. As time went on, and the calls continued without end, those little stones started to melt together in the heat of life. Pretty soon, I wasn't sure where that desire to help people had gone.

But God . . .

God found a way to seep life in between the stones to revive a heart so near to death, I probably could have been mistaken for the man on the emergency room table. Consider what God told His prophet, Ezekiel:

> And I will give you a new heart, and I will put a new spirit in you. I will take out your stony, stubborn heart and give you a tender, responsive heart. And I will put My Spirit in you so that you will follow My decrees and be careful to obey My regulations. (Ezekiel 36:26–27 (NLT))

The Lord graciously removed my hard heart and replaced it with one that is soft and moldable. He gave me a responsive heart that cares greatly for people again. Now, instead of just another "cop" doing the work that cops do, I was there for a very different purpose.

However, other than prayer, I didn't know what that purpose was at the time I was watching this drama unfold. It was by God's grace I was even at the hospital in the first place. God had moved mountains to get me there. And now I was being asked to go with the patient to another hospital where there was a specialist waiting to repair the worst of his injuries.

I watched flight-for-life come in, package him up, and lift off to fly to the other side of the metro area. I loved the way the helicopter rotors created the wind that struck me in the face as it lifted off. On a side note: I can never get over my amazement of flight.

It took forty-five minutes to get to the other hospital. The drive gave me a lot of time to get my heart right with the Lord. I prayed fervently for this man who had been injured so severely, yet whose life was still in his body. He was not out of the woods, but life is God's to do with what He wishes. No matter what happened in the next handful of hours, I knew God had His hands on him.

I remembered something that was written in Psalm 139 that supported this promise:

> For You formed my inward parts; You covered me in my mother's womb. I will praise You, for I am fearfully and wonderfully made; marvelous are Your works, and that my soul knows very well. My frame was not hidden from You, when I was made in secret, and skillfully wrought in the lowest parts of the earth. Your eyes saw my substance, being yet unformed. And in Your book they all were written, the days fashioned for me, when as yet there were none of them. (Psalm 139:13–16 (NKJV))

Oh my, how God knows everything about us. And in His Book of Life, He knows how long our days on Earth will be. It's important to remember that the One who gives life will keep us close to Himself until those days in His book are fulfilled.

I got to the hospital, and the patient was in surgery. Good. He survived the flight. Each subsequent step strengthened my faith that this was not going to be a recovery mission—he had a chance at life. By God's grace . . .

Four hours of surgery. Four hours in the break room. Four hours past my normal time to get off shift. And I was no closer to knowing the reason God wanted me there.

But God asks us to be patient. This is one thing I have to pray for, *a lot*. God asks us to walk in His will without wavering and to be obedient even when information isn't readily available. That takes trust.

Trust is defined as "reliance on the integrity, strength, ability, surety, of a person or thing; to have confidence in something or someone."[1] Often, the Lord doesn't tell us why He does something, and He usually doesn't tell us the outcome before we get to it. Trust in God ensures we follow Him even when we don't know where we are going. I had faith that there was a reason I was there. But all I could do was wait and trust.

Recently, I had been chewing on a Bible passage written by the Apostle Paul that details what it means to be a Christian. I was reading it again this week. That passage says:

> Don't just pretend to love others. Really love them. Hate what is wrong. Hold tightly to what is good. Love each other with genuine affection, and take delight in honoring each other. Never be lazy, but work hard and serve the Lord enthusiastically. Rejoice in our confident hope. Be patient in trouble, and keep on praying. When God's people are in need, be ready to help them. Always be eager to practice hospitality. (Romans 12:9–13 (NLT))

I was ready to honor God and help those in need as I was sitting there. But hours were going by without even a small opportunity. And then the text message came in.

One of the department's victim advocates sent me a text message to tell me that they had located the patient's mother. She lived in a different city than where the shooting of her son had happened. And she was headed to the hospital I was sitting in, which was also in another city, so no one had made face-to-face contact with her from our agency.

Now I wasn't trying to work out my replacement. Instead, I knew I was in the perfect place to be that contact for her. The love of Christ compelled me to stay and make that connection —to do exactly what Paul was talking about in Romans—to be a Christian.

Could it be God made the current call I had been trying to complete impossible to finish, so He could send me to this call, perfectly on time? Did He place each of those seven bullets in the man's body in such a way that he did not die when he probably should have? Could it be God then sent me to a hospital across the city—a location no other personnel from our department could go—for me to be in a place where I could show the love of Christ to a grieving mother? I think the answer is absolutely yes!

Before I go further, let's revisit the verses from the Book of Ezekiel, so we can see the purity and relevance of God's Word in this case:

> And I will give you a new heart, and I will put a new spirit in you. I will take out your stony, stubborn heart and give you a tender, responsive heart. And I will put my Spirit in you so that you will follow My decrees and be careful to obey My regulations. (Ezekiel 36:26–27 (NLT))

What's interesting about these verses is there are two sides to the coin. On one side, is the idea of having a heart so soft and usable by God, the difficulties in your life and others' lives, can truly cause discomfort.

I told you that God had slowly removed the stones from my heart, which had been weathered by too much hate, turmoil, and tragedy—hard things to deal with in my career. God had wrapped His loving arms around me and had shown me grace. He had given me His Spirit, which had matured me into a man of God so hungry that following God's leading was the only thing I wanted to do. But, in doing so, it had melted away the callous and uncaring shield I had relied on for so long, to keep me from becoming too emotionally invested in these difficult scenarios. I was hurting for the family, and no man should have to see this kind of stuff.

The other side of the coin is the person whose heart is so rocky and hard that life, in general, constricts any feelings that God exists and is in control. In essence, the hard, rocky exterior of a hard-hearted person feels no hope and sees no miracles from God.

As much as I was on one side of the coin, the grieving mother was on the other. After I listened to her inflamed anger about the man who had shot her son, a man now in police custody, she made it clear she would have no problem murdering the man and going to jail.

When I softly mentioned to her that God is the one who makes judgment for wrongs—"'Vengeance is Mine, I will repay,' says the Lord" (Romans 12:19 (NKJV)—she snapped back in anger. She told me, "I kicked God to the curb when He took my husband."

Suddenly, a grieving mother was also a grieving widow. I learned her husband had been sick for decades and had been taken from her only a few short months earlier. The little stones of life had melted together in her heart, and she had walked away from the only One who could provide the hope she needed.

I used the time to listen to her cry and hear about her husband, a retired police officer. It seemed it had been a while since she had been able to just "get it out." I also used the time to tell her about God's love for her and her son—the hope that she would find Jesus so she would see her husband again.

She told me that she hadn't received anything from God. I told her that I had witnessed at least three miracles from God since I had been added to the call. And one of them was me, sitting in front of her, telling her about it. I told her one of the most compelling pieces of evidence that exists to prove Jesus is real was me. He had saved me from a life of destruction and sin. And now, He was using me to share the love of Christ with her, in a different city than the one I even worked in.

Her eyes teared up and started to soften.

At this point, other family members started to come in, and I left for home. I still had another hour of work to do, and I wanted to get to bed. I had planted a seed into the hard ground of a hurting, grieving mother and wife. My prayer for her was to find herself back in God's loving arms and that her hard, stony heart would be replaced with a heart of flesh and the Holy Spirit.

What happens next for her isn't up to me. The Lord asks us to tell others about Him. The Bible says He will do the rest.

Man, this job is rewarding!

In another part of the world, there is a burial chamber where the dead should be lying. That chamber once had a large rock in front of it. But we learn in the Bible that when the rock was rolled away, they found no death. They only found life as Jesus had been raised from the dead. In essence, the rocky covering could not hold down the heart of life that was inside it.

And Jesus died and was risen so you could also be raised from the dead—from the death of sin in your life. My prayer for you is that you will roll away the stony door from your burial chamber. So, when we peer inside, we won't find your body there because you have been raised to life in Christ. This is the gospel of Jesus.

I would learn something the next day (after all of it was over), reaffirming God had handpicked me to be there. I talked to another officer who had been on the scene much earlier than me. Usually, we get an officer to the hospital as soon as we can to assess the patient. But when he volunteered to go, he was told no and was given another assignment.

When I finally got added to the call and asked where I was needed, the on-scene sergeant requested that I go get a report at the hospital. I thought it was a late assignment, but I wasn't going to argue. I know what the Holy Spirit, whom I carry with me always, brings to the table. And I felt I needed to take Him to the hospital. I also learned the victim advocate who had contacted me would have sent someone to meet with the grieving mother if it had been anyone other than me who was already there.

A week or two later, I shared this story with the victim advocate who then passed it along to that grieving mother and her now recovering son. I really hope God will invigorate a faith in Him that can only come from the speed bumps and potholes of life.

God had a plan—He *always* does.

17 / THE BASKETBALL
GOD'S GRACE OVERCOMES DIVISION

SOMETIMES, God calls us to the most unlikely of places. I was driving through a neighborhood after handling a simple call for service. It was late, but people were still awake and clamoring around the city. Most of the calls I handle are simple. But a violent riot was underway in our city, and it had been developing for a number of hours. I was intently listening to the radio traffic for any sign that I might be called in to assist.

As I told you in Chapter 2, what they say about police work is true. It's 99 percent boredom followed by 1 percent of sheer terror. It has always been that way. But in these new days of racial divide and social unrest, we are on edge more than we have ever been. This held true for the entire decade and a half that I had been policing in this wonderful city.

My heart was heavy—heavy for the war my brothers and sisters were fighting on the skirmish line of a protest that seemingly had no real value. We knew the battle was coming. And there were a decent number of agitators, bringing their masks, helmets, and weapons. Our department was ready.

I was working patrol behind them because life goes on outside the great lawn of our governmental buildings. That life is also full of lawlessness, pain, hurt, and anxiety. I wanted to be a part of the battle, standing on the line with those who wear the badge—those men and women I call my brothers and sisters in blue. But God had another purpose for me that night.

I was lackadaisically driving through the neighborhood on my way to the next call dispatch had sent me. My thoughts were far from the dangers that could be lurking around the next corner. Maybe that was my mistake. But it's hard to be hyper-vigilant all the time. It's truly exhausting.

I barely saw the object out of the corner of my eye as it crossed the path of my patrol SUV. It was grey and moving rapidly, entering from stage left. I couldn't swerve for fear of hitting the parked cars on the side of the street. I missed it with my front tires and then, *BOOM!*

I slammed on the brakes. I was certainly hyper-vigilant now! Any thoughts I had been entertaining were now focused on what that loud sound was.

It was the Fourth of July, and the area was full of colorful lights and deafening explosions from illegal fireworks. Man, they are loud. I never did any time in the military, so I often wondered what it sounds like as you listen to the sound of bombs and automatic small-arms fire ringing all around you. But what I heard and felt in my car was not a firework.

My job has trained me on firearms, and I have a pretty good idea of what they sound like. I know how loud they can be. But the only experience I have with a weapon being fired in my general direction was at a rodeo when the riders were shooting black powder pistols at balloons. I can tell you, from that experience, the sound of a gun fired *at* you is far louder than a gun you are shooting *away* from you. Having no real experience with that sort of thing, I wasn't sure if someone had shot at me from the shadows or not.

I quickly exited my patrol car. Being stuck in a box when you are being shot at is a bad thing. I looked to my left and saw a young, Black girl standing at the top of her driveway. I could tell by her posture—by the way her hands were clinging to one another, hanging in front of her, with her arms outstretched along the front of her body—that she was nervous.

I flashed a look back toward the rear of my patrol car. There, I saw the culprit of the loud sound that had scared me so badly. I had run over the young lady's basketball. The object I had seen come out into the street in front of me was just an errant rebound.

I looked back at her and took a deep breath. I took a few steps toward her. I called out to her that I was sorry for her ball, that I couldn't avoid it. I could tell she was afraid.

She yelled back, "It's okay. It has happened before." As she said it, she backed up into her driveway.

I'll be honest, I wasn't sure what to do at that moment. I had another call to get to, so I apologized again and drove away. But throughout the night, I thought about that ball and about the fear it had so suddenly caused me.

When we are placed in a perceived "life or death" situation, how do we react? These types of situations always come to us suddenly. When we aren't trained and haven't rehearsed in our minds what we would do, we often find out the hard way when faced with that situation. Thank the Lord that I learned very quickly that she was not a threat.

But what was that young lady thinking about me? Was I a threat to her? A White police officer had perceived a young Black teenager as a threat because the sound of her popping ball put me on edge.

A lot of the fears and anxieties we have about each other are real. And I have tried to ease those feelings of fear in many people over my career. In my mind, I have never posed that kind of threat to anyone as a police officer, no matter your ethnicity. But we live in a culture where others who wish to write a new narrative are causing these stress fractures to grow.

How was she feeling about what had happened? I had no idea.

Throughout the rest of the night, the Lord urged me to build a bridge. He brought me to the decision that I was going to replace her ball and, hopefully, replace her fear with a positive experience.

It was late, and all the stores were closed. I had to be patient. I hoped to take care of it the next day. I didn't think much more about it. Little did I know that all of this was going to play a tremendous part in the young girl's life.

What does Jesus desire of us when He says, "You shall love your neighbor as yourself" (Matthew 22:39 (NKJV))?

For context and to truly see the heart of God in this commandment, we should back up and see the rest of this conversation. The Bible says:

> Then one of them, a lawyer, asked Him a question, testing Him, and saying, "Teacher, which is the great commandment in the law?"

Jesus said to him, "'You shall love the LORD your God with all your heart, with all your soul, and with all your mind.' This is the first and great commandment. And the second is like it: 'You shall love your neighbor as yourself.' On these two commandments hang all the Law and the Prophets." (Matthew 22:35–40 (NKJV))

After the Jewish religious leadership had inflated the "law" to more than 600 individual laws governing every part of life, Jesus made a startling statement. He told the Jewish leaders that the entire law of Moses and everything the prophets of old had written came down to two laws: love God and love others.

And that makes sense. Although God provided Moses with the law, it was never to be used to oppress His people. God simply wanted His people to act with the same heart He had for them.

So, who are our neighbors? And what does God say about loving them? It's certainly safe to say this young lady is not my physical neighbor, she lives nowhere near me. In fact, in the scheme of things, I really don't have that many neighbors. So why does Jesus make this commandment so important?

The word *neighbor* is defined as "one living or located near another."[1] However, the word used in the Greek language is *plesion*. Although the English translators use the word *neighbor*, the word *plesion* has a broader and more inclusive definition than the word *neighbor* has in the English language. The word *plesion* gives the idea that *everyone* is your neighbor.[2]

No matter where they live or how they look, no matter where their ancestors came from or how light or dark the shade of their skin, we are all neighbors. And Jesus put the love of our neighbors just below the love we should have for God. Jesus says we should love others as we love ourselves. And you know how selfish we can be with loving ourselves.

But the Apostle Paul takes it up a notch when he wrote:

> Is there any encouragement from belonging to Christ? Any comfort from His love? Any fellowship together in the Spirit? Are your hearts tender and compassionate? Then make me truly happy by agreeing wholeheartedly with each other, loving one another, and working together with one mind and purpose.

> Don't be selfish; don't try to impress others. Be humble, thinking of others as better than yourselves. Don't look out only for your own interests, but take an interest in others, too. (Philippians 2:1–4 (NLT))

Paul continues on in this passage of Scripture by illustrating how Jesus Christ, who is our glorious God, came to Earth, putting on flesh, so He could be wholly human. He gave away all His glory and His wealth so He could become a humble servant. In doing so, Jesus looked on all His creation—all the people He made in His image—as higher than Himself. And He came to sacrifice His own life so we could live in communion with God.

The Bible calls this type of love, *agape* love. This kind of love is poignantly described by Paul in his first letter to the Corinthian church.

> Love [agape] is patient and kind. Love is not jealous or boastful or proud or rude. It does not demand its own way. It is not irritable, and it keeps no record of being wronged. It does not rejoice about injustice but rejoices whenever the

truth wins out. Love never gives up, never loses faith, is always hopeful, and endures through every circumstance. (1 Corinthians 13:4–7 (NLT))

Agape love is a love that seeks nothing in return and holds no grudges. This love is color-blind and seeks the good in everyone. It's a love that forgives quickly and respects life—a love that gives more than it takes and drives us to sacrifice our own wants for the needs of others.

That kind of sacrificial love, love that is known as *agape* love, is what Jesus had in mind when He told us to love our neighbors (all people) as ourselves. That was the kind of love Jesus had in mind when He allowed Himself to be beaten, scourged, and nailed to a Roman cross. It was *that* kind of love that led me to build a bridge with this young lady and her family.

I got into my patrol car the next day, and I initiated a call for service at her address so I wouldn't get caught up in something else. This call was incredibly important to me. I punched in the needed information and submitted it.

My screen updated me to a call at her address. I glanced at the incident number, information that is usually not that important. But the number stopped my heart for a brief moment. I was looking at incident number ****01111.

Let me explain. At this point, I had been pouring my life into God's will for five years. Ever since I came up out of the water during my baptism, God had taken hold of my life in ways I could not have ever dreamed. The badge I wear is nothing more than a key—a pass to get me into places where people are hurting to give agape love to others. Over that time, I have noticed God speaks to me in many ways. One of those ways is through the number 1111. I knew God was in the details.

I knocked on the door. When the family answered, I asked to speak to the girl who . . .

"Had her ball run over?" her mother asked. I said yes.

She called the young lady to the door as if she was in trouble. I immediately recognized the scared teenager from the night before. She looked just as anxious.

I handed her the gift card I had purchased on the way to her house. I told her that I wanted to replace her basketball—her favorite ball, as I would later find out. At this, her face lit up, and she took the card from me, telling me thank you.

We talked about the incident a little—how loud the sound was and how much it had scared her. She asked if she could give me a hug. I said, "Of course."

That scared young lady gave me a hug that lasted no less than fifteen seconds, an embrace I felt had a deeper meaning behind it. I was fighting back tears as I felt her energy in the tightness of her hug. It reminded me of Jesus when He said:

> "Who touched Me?"
>
> When all denied it, Peter and those with him said, "Master, the multitudes throng and press You, and You say, 'Who touched Me?'"
>
> But Jesus said, "Somebody touched Me, for I perceived power going out from Me." (Luke 8:45–46 (NKJV))

Jesus was so in tune with what was going on around Him that He knew when someone's touch was different. That is exactly what I felt. I knew there was more behind the girl's hug. It felt like energy came into me. And throughout the rest of my shift, I dwelled on it.

I finally came to the conclusion that I needed to dig for answers. As it turned out, and without any planning on my part, I made a phone call to her mother at 11:11 p.m. After I fumbled through the unconventional reason I was calling, how God had led me through the number 1111, and how He had led me through the evening's events, what I learned from her mother was truly amazing.

The teenager's mother told me after the ball popped and she came inside, the fear was felt greatly in the house. Everyone heard the loud sound. They thought it was a gunshot because it was so different than the other fireworks in the area.

She told me that she had never feared for the lives of her children until that night. She said, in this new, very divisive, and tense culture, the outcome could have been radically different. She feared a perfect storm where a police officer, anxious for his safety, would defend himself not knowing what was going on. In that scenario, the current race-relations issue would not have been helpful.

Then she told me that her daughter had always dreamed of being a police officer. But after the circumstances in the nation and the media that led to all of this turmoil, she had become disheartened with the police and had put her dreams on the shelf. Her mother wouldn't expound too much into her daughter's life. But she told me, "With all she has been through, what you did and your hug will have more of an effect on her than you will ever know. It was huge what you did."

I hung up the phone, fighting back tears. I praised God in heaven for what He had done, both in and through my life.

The small sacrifice I had made financially, and the agape love I had been driven to display to someone I had only met a few hours before, had been used to further God's kingdom.

I believe God, through His providence (control of all things), had made the ball skip across the street and had popped it under my tires to set off a cascade of obedient decisions, so a bridge could be built between a young, Black teenage girl and a White police officer . . . and between heaven and Earth.

As Jesus prayed:

> Your kingdom come. Your will be done on earth as it is in heaven. (Matthew 6:10 (NKJV))

God's kingdom came to Earth yesterday in the eye of a young girl. And I felt the glory of heaven.

Love . . . there's nothing else to say.

I LOVE the versatility of the Bible. There are so many teachings of Jesus that can be applied in different ways. Just like when I'm investigating a situation at work, there are many people, all with different vantage points. Each of those vantage points has value, and there is always a lesson to be learned.

Take the Parable of the Sower for instance. In the Book of Mark, Jesus uses a parable—a fictional story that carries a strong spiritual truth—to illustrate His heart and the ways Christians can further the kingdom of heaven here on the earth.

Historically, when this parable has been taught, most people lock in on the importance of the different kinds of soils. As a review, let me refresh your memory:

> "Listen! Behold, a sower went out to sow. And it happened, as he sowed, that some seed fell by the wayside; and the birds of the air came and devoured it. Some fell on stony ground, where it did not have much earth; and immediately it sprang up because it had no depth of earth. But when the sun was up it was scorched, and because it had no root it withered

away. And some seed fell among thorns; and the thorns grew up and choked it, and it yielded no crop. But other seed fell on good ground and yielded a crop that sprang up, increased and produced: some thirtyfold, some sixty, and some a hundred."

And He said to them, "He who has ears to hear, let him hear!" (Mark 4:3–9 (NKJV))

In a predominately agrarian culture, this parable spoke powerfully to those who were listening. And later in the chapter, Jesus explained this parable to His disciples.

And He said to them, "Do you not understand this parable? How then will you understand all the parables?

The sower sows the word. And these are the ones by the wayside where the word is sown. When they hear, Satan comes immediately and takes away the word that was sown in their hearts.

These likewise are the ones sown on stony ground who, when they hear the word, immediately receive it with gladness; and they have no root in themselves, and so endure only for a time. Afterward, when tribulation or persecution arises for the word's sake, immediately they stumble.

Now these are the ones sown among thorns; they are the ones who hear the word, and the cares of this world, the deceitfulness of riches, and the desires for other things entering in choke the word, and it becomes unfruitful.

But these are the ones sown on good ground, those who hear the word, accept it, and bear fruit: some thirtyfold, some sixty, and some a hundred." (Mark 4:13–20 (NKJV))

When a parable has a direct passage in the Bible to interpret its meaning, we know the issue is settled by the words of Jesus. The main teaching of this parable is to illustrate the different kinds of soils—the different types of hearts that receive the Word of God. Yet, I can see another layer that we can learn from.

It's a layer not investigated by Jesus in this writing, but I can see God's heart in it, nonetheless. And it would have never caught my attention if not for a wonderful story of growth and restoration God placed in my lap, a letter I received that changed everything.

Before I tell this story, let me introduce you to the conventional interpretation of this parable. We love to speak about the different kinds of soils we believe hold our hearts.

There is the rocky soil that places our hearts in a shallow relationship with God. When life gets hard and persecution comes, that shallow relationship tends to fade away.

Then there's the soil laden with weeds and thorns. The heart finds growth through accepting the Word of God. But then the sustenance in the soil is stolen away by imposters (weeds)—the cares and concerns of the world and its riches—and faith withers away.

Next, we see there are always those hard soils that don't even let God's Word take root at all. In those cases, Satan tends to snatch that seed away completely, so those who hear the Word never even believe in God at all.

But then there's the good, fertile soil that allows the gospel to bury itself deep—to develop strong roots that can bear blessings (fruit) and weather any storm. This is the soil that bears the most fruit for the kingdom of God.

Jesus told us this was the way to interpret the parable. And if we're paying attention, we probably know different people who possess each of these soils. It's important to know where your heart is when you read, pray, and meditate in God's presence. This parable truly makes a wonderful teaching tool.

Yet, what if we stopped for a moment and looked, not at the types of soils, but at the sower? The parable clearly says, "The sower sows the word" (Mark 4:14 (NKJV)). To be a sower in farming circles, you would have to be involved in the casting and planting of seeds. A sower "sows" seeds into a garden or field.

In fact, the word *sow* means "to plant seed for growth especially by scattering."[1] To take it one step further, the definition of *scatter* is "to separate and go in various directions; disperse" and "to occur or fall irregularly or at random."[2]

Based on these definitions, you should get a picture of a man carelessly throwing seeds all over the field in which he is sowing. He doesn't care what kind of soil it is. Maybe it's because, to his naked eye, he doesn't take into consideration the value of the soil on which the seeds are landing. Or maybe he doesn't really know which seeds will sprout and bear the fruit he is seeking as a farmer.

If we take a very plain look at the parable, Jesus is describing a man who is dispersing the Word of God in the same way—wildly, all over the place. You certainly get the picture that the sower is not worried too much about where his teaching is going or who is hearing it. He just wants to cover as many hearts as he can, not knowing who might be changed by it.

So, as a police officer and a man who wishes to be a sower of the Word, I tended to cast the seeds of God's Word everywhere I went. As you can imagine, I met a lot of people in the midst of their worst days. And in my heart, I knew I had comfort and maybe even the solution to what was ailing their hearts.

This was important because the badge I proudly wore gave me access to "fields" to which no one else might have access. And sowing the Word of God might be just the thing people needed for incredible change and healing in their lives. But I had found that, since I didn't know the condition of people's hearts, I needed to wildly sow the Word to everyone I met.

God speaks to this truth in the Book of First Samuel. It's an important principle, and there are many facets of its application. So, let's pause for a minute to make sure we understand it.

To give you a little background, the prophet Samuel, at God's leading, was looking for the next king of Israel. God had sent him to a certain house where one of the sons of the homeowner would be God's choice for the next king. But God did something interesting: He didn't tell Samuel who he was looking for ahead of time.

The homeowner, Jesse, had eight sons. And God told Samuel:

> Take a heifer with you, and say, "I have come to sacrifice to the LORD." Then invite Jesse to the sacrifice, and I will show you what you shall do; you shall anoint for Me the one I name to you. (1 Samuel 16:2–3 (NKJV))

God told Samuel to step out in faith and go to Jesse's house. God said He would make His choice known when it was the right time.

This is just like the sower. If we waited around for God to tell us exactly where the seed should be planted, we wouldn't be acting in faith. Instead, God only gives us the next step, desiring us to take it so He can reveal the next one. So, let's see what happened when Samuel got there.

> So it was, when they came, that he looked at Eliab and said, "Surely the LORD's anointed is before Him!"

> But the LORD said to Samuel, "Do not look at his appearance or at his physical stature, because I have refused him. For the LORD does not see as man sees; for man looks at the outward appearance, but the LORD looks at the heart." (1 Samuel 16:6–7 (NKJV))

Jesse presented each of his seven sons that he had brought to the feast, and the Lord rejected them all. None of them had the heart of a king. As it turned out, God's choice was for the son whom Jesse hadn't even brought—the one that he and his brothers were ashamed of, the one left back at the house to tend the sheep.

That son's name was David. Samuel was left to work his way through each son, not knowing anything about them ahead of time. He waited patiently until he met David, and God told Samuel that it was the heart of David that He had chosen as king.

This Bible passage illustrates a simple truth: we cannot know how the seeds of God will affect the hearts of men. Therefore, scatter the Word of God, the heart of God, and the love of God to everyone you meet. I had no idea this truth was about to come full circle in my life.

The briefing ended as it always did, and we were getting ready to load up for another shift. Police work these days is tumultuous at best. And we spend a lot of our time, worrying about our safety plans and other such concerns.

I was standing in the parking lot when I was approached by a fellow officer. "Did you see the letter on the table in briefing?" "No," I said.

I didn't make it a habit of looking at anything on the front table. I figured if it hadn't been read to the shift by the watch commander, then it wasn't that important. The officer told me the letter detailed the actions of an unidentified officer, and he wanted to know if it was me. He then said it would make sense after I read the letter.

The two-page, typewritten letter appeared to be haphazardly put together, as if it had been an afterthought. I read through the contents. The letter detailed the heartbreak and difficulties a young woman had suffered at the hands of her now ex-boyfriend, and later on, the courts. She talked about how she knew her very young daughter had been a victim of sexual abuse at her ex-boyfriend's hands and how she could find no way to prove it. Domestic violence and other heart-wrenching situations had brought her to the point of attempting suicide.

It was hard to read. But then, I came to the following line:

I'm writing this letter because it was heavy on my heart. The world hates you. I'm a Black woman and when my life was falling apart and I was thinking about ending it successfully, this time, you knocked on my door to pray. You have no idea the kind of faith in humanity you restored for me that day. I decided to fight.

The other officer said, "Was that you? I don't know anyone else who prays for people or who does that sort of thing around here."

The letter was signed, "Candace." I didn't recognize her name. I would have to look back at police resources to figure it out. But as I was standing there with the letter, a third officer said, "What an honor it is to be the first one someone thinks of when associated with this kind of thing."

God had placed that letter on the table and had shown it to one of the few officers who had actually been on a call with me when I prayed for someone in distress. And to be the one who crossed his mind when he read that an unknown officer had prayed for the author . . .

How important it is to shine the light of Christ to everyone we meet—to everyone we work around. You truly don't know who is paying attention.

Jesus said it this way:

> You are the light of the world. A city that is set on a hill cannot be hidden. Nor do they light a lamp and put it under a basket, but on a lampstand, and it gives light to all who are in the house. Let your light so shine before men, that they may see your good works and glorify your Father in heaven. (Matthew 5:14–16 (NKJV))

In her letter, Candace went on to describe the miraculous changes in her life, which hinged upon that day. She closed her letter by saying:

> *The job you do is NOT easy. One wrong or fast move and someone's life is changed forever. You guys are good people.*

During that rough time, I met [almost] the whole station. I just want you to remember that you are human too, and everyone is not against you. I will always remember the officer praying with me, even if I don't remember his name. The smallest things make the biggest difference. Thank you for everything you do.

I looked into the archives to find I had been one of three officers who had been to her house in the darkest hours of her life. Amazingly, I learned the whole incident had occurred a little more than two years before. She had left details of the miraculous changes God had made in her life, and she had left her phone number.

I called Candace to get more—to reach out to praise God along with her for His faithfulness in her life. Over the next fifteen minutes or so, I would learn about the incredible blessings that had come from God's healing over the last two years. She told me after the three of us had made contact with her and after the prayer I had taken the time to pray with her the next day, a chain reaction of healing had begun—a chain reaction of God's blessings in her life.

Now, she runs an organization that helps women who are victims of the same things she suffered from. My heart swelled at witnessing God's glory and provision as she told me how her life had turned around for the good. I could see how the seeds I had planted from God's Word had truly sprouted in the fertile soil of her heart and had blossomed into life-giving fruit in others' lives.

I told Candace that I was blessed by her taking the time to write the letter because I don't get to see God's work in the lives of those I pray for very often. She said she "just felt compelled to say something." By the end of the conversation, we were both in tears. God is so good!

The Bible tells us that God's work is

> to console those who mourn in Zion, to give them beauty for ashes, the oil of joy for mourning, the garment of praise for the spirit of heaviness; that they may be called trees of righteousness, the planting of the LORD, that He may be glorified, (Isaiah 61:3 (NKJV))

and to

> restore to you the years that the swarming locust has eaten. (Joel 2:25 (NKJV))

God wants us to come alongside the growth He is doing in people's lives. He wants us to be part of his restoration—the beauty that comes out of the ashes of despair, the gladness that comes out of mourning, and to restore the years of destruction that has chewed up the lives of others.

But as Samuel learned, we cannot judge the soils where we cast the seeds of His Word. We cannot see the hearts of others. So we must wildly cast the seeds of God's love on every type of soil we find. You never know, the loving embrace of our Lord and Savior, Jesus Christ, might make those seeds, and your words, the swinging point that changes the lives of those who find themselves in your path of "sowing."

19 / IA INVESTIGATION

GOD'S GRACE ALLOWS TRIALS TO MAKE YOU STRONGER

And the Lord said, "Simon, Simon! Indeed, Satan has asked for you, that he may sift you as wheat." (Luke 22:31 (NKJV))

THERE COMES a time in the life of every believer when a conversation like this occurs. When something happens that decimates us and tests us to our very core. Although you probably won't hear Jesus audibly say this to you, we have the idea plainly written in the Scriptures for us to ingest, chew on, and ultimately suffer through when it happens.

God's Word is written for our learning. The Bible is a tremendous help in navigating our trials and tribulations. It has the power to transform us so fundamentally that we will change the way we live our lives once we've become new creations in Christ (2 Corinthians 5:17).

Recently, I've found myself meditating on a time when I was "sifted as wheat." It was a level of testing I had never faced before. And when it was over—when I walked out of the sifter —I came out with nothing. And I came out with *everything*.

But first, let me give you some context.

In the ancient agrarian, Hebrew culture, farming wheat was a way of life. After harvesting the wheat stalks, a farmer would separate the useful grain from the unnecessary chaff. This was a brutal and violent action. The grain was pulled from the stalk and collected. Then, what was left over was thrown into the fire.

The edible grain grows in a protective casing that must be removed. But that casing is very hard. It must be violently crushed and beaten into pieces, so the valuable grain can be collected from inside.

Afterward, the piles of broken wheat kernels are separated in a sifter. The screens allow the valuable stuff to fall through while the broken pieces of the protective shells are discarded. Although much of the activity is mechanized today, the wheat harvesting actions have remained largely unchanged since ancient times.

God, in His unsurpassed wisdom, uses this simple illustration to show us just how much our souls are like a single kernel of wheat in His field. He draws a picture of our development toward the fruitful life He has already planned for us.

We have an internal value that God wants to harvest. But in this life on Earth, He must first break through the tough, outer shell of self-protection, pride, arrogance, self-sufficiency, and disobedience. And the only way the Lord can find that beautiful "you" that is hiding inside, is to crush it, beat it, and separate the shell from you.

One day, I walked into a department store on a call about a shoplifter in custody. When I was ushered into that little office —the one I have stood in no less than a hundred times in my almost two-decade career—it was just like every other call I had been on. The young lady took some merchandise and was caught by a loss prevention employee when she attempted to leave without paying for it.

It was an open-and-shut case. I was pretty sure I could write this report in the dark . . . until I checked her purse for weapons and found a small amount of methamphetamine. Okay, still no big deal. I've done that too.

But by this point in my career, I had found my true relationship with God. After being saved from myself and my sins, and after I started pulling really close to Jesus, I started to see the people I was dealing with in a very different way. I saw them as valuable souls, not just the "beans" that were to be counted.

I mean, how can I be a hypocrite? After Jesus pulled me back from my own horrible, near-life-long addiction, I knew there was so much more to people—the people whom God had made in His own image. And I knew well that an arrest and criminal charges rarely change anyone for the better. I had resolved to look for better ways to end the cycle.

However, this put me in an interesting predicament. Boy, am I glad I'm not God. Because, unlike God who can make dual decisions, I had to decide between justice and mercy. In my human mind, I couldn't choose both.

So instead of completing the cookie-cutter, color-by-number approach to police work I had implemented for these types of things in the past, I decided to do a deeper investigation. I wanted to see whether her statement that "it's not mine, it's my boyfriend's" was actually true. I would have greatly appreciated the same kind of courtesy if I had been in the same position, one where I was wrongfully punished for something I didn't do.

A time-consuming investigation found that this young lady had no documented criminal history of drug use. In her purse were a men's pair of glasses and a set of contact lenses. There was also a bag of syringes, along with the aforementioned drugs, enough for multiple uses.

I checked and found no evidence of needle marks on her arms or burns on her lips. She was a healthy weight and was in her right mind as I spoke to her. She provided her "abusive" boyfriend's name and date of birth, hoping I would look into his past to prove her innocence.

He was easy to find. Well-known in our city, he was a meth dealer and had multiple charges for selling drugs. He showed a history of meth use; the intravenous kind.

She told me that he always made her carry his "belongings" in her purse but didn't know the items were there since she had not been with him all day. And the last bit of the story—she was a single mother of a six-year-old daughter.

- *Justice says*: she is in possession of illegal substances so she should be punished. The law is the law.

- *Mercy says*: she seems to be telling me a true story based on the evidence (or lack thereof). Therefore, a little grace should be extended to keep her out of jail and get her home to her daughter.

Since the Lord came into my life, I have tried to live by the following rule: if you are going to make a mistake, err on the side of grace.

After I prayed about it several times, and after listening for the moving of the Holy Spirit in my heart, that's what I did. I showed mercy and grace.

I charged her with what I could clearly prove: shoplifting. And I let her go on the arrestable drug possession charge because I didn't want her to be punished for someone else's dirty deeds. I collected the drugs and put them into evidence for destruction and wrote a complete report, so there would be no question about what I had done. Easy as that.

And then came the grain sifter—and a six-month period that would ultimately change my life.

When Jesus told the prideful Apostle Peter (Simon) that Satan had asked for him, Peter must have thought, *Say what*? But there is so much to learn about Jesus, Satan, Peter, and us when we look at this story of crushing, beating, and separating.

Jesus didn't just tell Peter that he would be sifted like wheat. He said:

> Simon, Simon! Indeed, Satan has asked for you, that he may sift you as wheat. But I have prayed for you, that your faith should not fail; and when you have returned to Me, strengthen your brethren. (Luke 22:31–32 (NKJV))

No doubt Peter's blood ran cold when Jesus said this. I'm sure he knew exactly what being "sifted" entailed. He likely had pictures of the large stones crushing the pods into bits. He probably knew people who had their hands crushed under the weight of those mighty stones. It couldn't have been a pleasant thought.

But Peter, in his pride, responded:

Lord, I am ready to go with You, both to prison and to death. (Luke 22:33 (NKJV))

Peter was ready to take on the "sifting" he figured was the most likely outcome. The religious leaders had pegged Jesus and His Apostles as "zealots." And I'm sure the scuttle on the street was they were probably facing imprisonment and death. I have to think Peter was driven by a sense of misdirected toughness—one that warriors have in their hearts that would see imprisonment and death as the ultimate noble outcome of a life spent fighting a worthy cause.

I stand behind the badge, unashamed of this feeling of honor too. In that misguided zeal, Peter took on the entire Roman arrest party, cutting off Malchus's right ear, in defense of his Lord (John 18:10). He was ready; he said it all the time.

But Jesus had something else in mind. Far from what Peter expected, Jesus had a very different lesson He wanted to develop in Peter—one he didn't see coming.

As it turned out, Jesus had something "way out of left field" in mind for me too. I didn't think another thing about that silly theft call. I even got into the car, and I prayed that this young lady would get out of her abusive relationship and raise her daughter in a better environment. I felt I had done the right thing. Even more importantly, I felt I had done what the Lord had led me to do.

I pride myself on always doing the right thing. But the confidence I was holding was ruffled when my sergeant pulled me aside and asked me why I didn't make an arrest. I believed in my heart Satan was reacting to my obedience in showing mercy in this case. So, I defended my actions.

We must always expect the enemy will put up a countermeasure when we obey God. I proudly told my boss the reasons I made my decision—a decision that was not against the law, a decision I had the discretion to make, and a decision I felt was the right thing to do. My supervisor knew I followed Jesus. Although he told me that he didn't agree, he said he understood my decision and approved my report.

I didn't think any more about it when my direct supervisor did not order me to do anything else. Thank you, Lord, for your guidance. It feels good to care for people, even those who break the law. This was what I thought Jesus wanted to teach me. Lesson learned Lord, thank you!

I kind of felt like Peter when he proudly proclaimed he would go to jail and die for Jesus. But then Jesus dropped the bomb on Peter—that is, Jesus allowed Peter to be tested in an unpredictable way.

And then about 2,000 years later, He dropped the bomb on me too—a test against something I could have never predicted. And in our collective pride, neither of us saw it coming. The Bible says:

> Jesus said to him, "Assuredly, I say to you that today, even this night, before the rooster crows twice, you will deny Me three times." (Mark 14:30 (NKJV); *see also* Luke 22:34)

Ouch! This statement cut Peter straight to the heart. No longer was this "sifting" a rock Peter would stand proudly on, proclaiming his will to die *for* his Lord. Instead, it was now quicksand that showed Peter would be a coward, denying he even knew Jesus to save himself *from* being killed for his Lord.

From here, the night moved quickly. And Peter denied the Lord three times, just as Jesus had prophetically proclaimed.

> Now as Peter was below in the courtyard, one of the servant girls of the high priest came. And when she saw Peter warming himself, she looked at him and said, "You also were with Jesus of Nazareth."
>
> But he denied it, saying, "I neither know nor understand what you are saying." And he went out on the porch, and a rooster crowed.
>
> And the servant girl saw him again, and began to say to those who stood by, "This is one of them." But he denied it again.
>
> And a little later those who stood by said to Peter again, "Surely you are one of them; for you are a Galilean, and your speech shows it."
>
> Then he began to curse and swear, "I do not know this Man of whom you speak!"
>
> A second time the rooster crowed. Then Peter called to mind the word that Jesus had said to him, "Before the rooster crows twice, you will deny Me three times." And when he thought about it, he wept. (Mark 14:66–72 (NKJV))

In an instant of fear, Peter completely denied knowing the Man for whom he had earlier said he would die. Another gospel describes how Peter and Jesus locked eyes after the rooster crowed (Luke 22:61). And I'm sure Peter's heart sank . . .

Crush, beat, separate. Peter's sifting had begun.

And a few weeks later, so did mine. I found a white envelope in my mailbox. Although I had never received one like this before, I knew exactly what it was. I had counseled and encouraged other officers when they received theirs. It was a summons from internal affairs.

I learned my cover officer that night, an officer with whom I had been in some pretty heated disagreements, had gone to my sergeant to complain about how I completed my investigation. That sergeant—my sergeant—the one who had initially approved my actions, told me several weeks later that he would have kept it at his level, but he had no choice.

Looking at his signature on the initial letter of complaint, it was hard not to feel betrayed at that moment. He had a chance to keep it at his level by doing his job. All he had to do was order me to do something different.

But now the little fix was a big problem for my heart. I felt betrayed. And that guy who pressed to do everything right— that guy who felt he could boast about never doing anything wrong and who had been in trouble fewer times than he could count, even back in his younger days—was facing disciplinary action for doing something that was well within his discretion to do.

Satan had asked Jesus to sift me. Jesus had said yes. And Satan attacked me at my most sacred place: my integrity. My heart sank.

Crush, beat, separate. My sifting had begun.

Before I continue my story, let's take a closer look at Luke 22:31. Did you notice that Jesus told Peter (Simon) that Satan actually *asked* to sift him?

Does it send chills up your spine like it does mine to think that Satan and Jesus communicate? Or that Satan, the evil lord of this world, even has the opportunity to ask permission from the King of the universe to do something? Even more chilling and more importantly: Doesn't it seem crazy that Jesus would even entertain the notion?

We have always been led to believe they are mortal enemies. But would it change your thoughts to learn Satan (Lucifer) is as much a created being as you and me? Granted, there will come a day when Satan will be destroyed. He will be judged for his wickedness like those who fail to accept Jesus in the human realm. Yet, this passage is telling. A short study of the Scriptures will uncover other places where interactions between God and Satan occurred.

In the Book of Job, we learn more about the relationship between God and Satan. There, we read that Job's life was the center of two discussions between God and Satan (Job 1:6–12, 2:1–7). What's unsettling to our hearts is to see God's willingness to allow Satan to decimate Job's life in order to prove Job's righteousness before God.

In the first two chapters, all of Job's children die, and he loses his personal possessions and good health. The only stipulation God put on Satan's actions was that he must not kill Job. How far can you go and how much can you lose before all you have is your life? Yet, we find that in Job's "crushing"—in the "sifting"—he never cursed God. He questioned God, but he never blamed Him.

So, let's look at Peter again.

Jesus told Peter that Satan had asked to "sift" him like wheat. Jesus then told Peter, "But I have prayed for you, that your faith should not fail" (Luke 22:32 (NKJV)). In this one response back to Peter, Jesus implied that He had given Satan permission to test him—to drag him through the mud, to place him in the fire.

Notice that Jesus didn't tell Satan no. He also didn't tell Peter, "Don't worry Peter, you're a Christian now, so I will protect you from Satan for the rest of your life." He didn't tell Peter, "Boy, if you only had more faith in Me, I would have told him to go home. Bummer . . ."

No, Jesus advised Peter that He had a conversation with Satan, without his knowledge, and He had given Satan permission to bring the "pain." But Jesus then uttered the most wonderful words that Peter, you, and I could ever hear. He said, "I have prayed for you."

The Bible says Jesus is our great High Priest. It tells us that Jesus, the Son of God, came as a human so He would understand what we go through here on Earth.

I think this is an amazing truth. The Creator of all things knows what it's like to be tired, thirsty, and hungry. He knows how it feels to be sad enough to weep and obedient enough to die. In fact, look at what the Bible tells us about Jesus. It was Christ Jesus

> who, being in the form of God, did not consider it robbery to be equal with God, but made Himself of no reputation, taking the form of a bondservant, and coming in the likeness of men. And being found in appearance as a man, He humbled Himself and became obedient to the point of death, even the death of the cross. (Philippians 2:6–8 (NKJV))

I think it's amazing that our Savior knows what it feels like to be sifted. It happened at an incredibly intense level when Satan sifted Jesus in the desert (Matthew 4:1–11). He knows how it feels to be Peter . . . and me . . . and you, too! The Bible comforts me greatly by saying:

> For we do not have a High Priest who cannot sympathize with our weaknesses, but was in all points tempted as we are, yet without sin. Let us therefore come boldly to the throne of grace, that we may obtain mercy and find grace to help in time of need. (Hebrews 4:15–16 (NKJV))

The God of the universe came down here to find out what it's like to be us. And because He knows this, He can effectively pray back to the Father on our behalf when we are sifted . . . beaten . . . broken . . . depressed . . . anxious . . . or tempted.

The Bible says, as the great High Priest, Jesus is the Mediator between us and the Father. He is our advocate, and He is our Counselor in heavenly affairs. There is no one better than Jesus when it comes down to it.

It seemed like forever as I waited for all of it to trickle down to me. There is nothing more revealing than waiting. I love what Jeremiah says in the Book of Lamentations, a section of Scripture I visited many a time during my sifting:

> My soul still remembers and sinks within me. This I recall to my mind, therefore I have hope.

> Through the LORD's mercies we are not consumed, because His compassions fail not. They are new every morning; great is Your faithfulness. "The LORD is my portion," says my soul, "Therefore I hope in Him!"

The LORD is good to those who wait for Him, to the soul who seeks Him. It is good that one should hope and wait quietly for the salvation of the LORD. It is good for a man to bear the yoke in his youth.

Let him sit alone and keep silent, because God has laid it on him; let him put his mouth in the dust—there may yet be hope. Let him give his cheek to the one who strikes him, and be full of reproach.

For the Lord will not cast off forever. Though He causes grief, yet He will show compassion according to the multitude of His mercies. For He does not afflict willingly, nor grieve the children of men. (Lamentations 3:20–33 (NKJV))

The waiting game was full of prayer, tears, and pain. The self-righteous and self-sufficient "me" was being stripped away. The things I held on to so tightly in my own strength were easily being removed, as if I had no strength at all. The taste of dust and gravel was in my teeth. I waited . . . and waited.

Crushed, beaten, sifted . . .

During what seemed like an exceedingly long period of time, I had waited, been interviewed, received advice, been put off, been pushed back, been rescheduled, and sat alone pondering the fate of my career. My heart had been completely crushed, pulverized, and stripped away. The cool, confident, and self-righteous shell I had been wearing around for almost fifteen years on "the beat," lay on the floor.

Who was I, after pulling away all the useless "chaff" and the protective shells? Who was I, who lay exposed after the sifting process?

I believe it was the "new" me—a new creation—made in Christ. I was that little lamb, draped across the shoulders of the good Shepherd, knowing my broken leg would heal and I would feel free to be more and more dependent on Him.

When I understood I could do nothing at all in my own power, that I was at the mercy of the Lord Himself, I began to lean on Jesus more. This reminded me of Paul when he wrote:

> For we do not want you to be ignorant, brethren, of our trouble which came to us in Asia: that we were burdened beyond measure, above strength, so that we despaired even of life. Yes, we had the sentence of death in ourselves, that we should not trust in ourselves but in God who raises the dead, who delivered us from so great a death, and does deliver us; in whom we trust that He will still deliver us . . . .
> (2 Corinthians 1:8–10 (NKJV))

Plainly put, Paul had been so greatly sifted in that time that he and his friends had feared for their lives every day. But the continuous fear of death led them to trust God. What they found was God delivered them from all sorts of trials and tribulations; God was continuing to deliver them even as he was writing the letter; and God was expected, through faith, to protect them into the future.

The police association provided me with an attorney—one who sounded much like a Charlie Brown teacher. I talked to him for a little while but denied his services. I had my great High Priest with me when I finally stood before the police chief.

You cannot stop a man who has so much faith in his God, that even tribulation and death cannot faze him. Paul says in another place, "But none of these things move me; nor do I count my life dear to myself, so that I may finish my race with joy . . ." (Acts 20:24 (NKJV)).

After Jesus restored Peter's faith and healed the damage Peter had done to his own heart, Jesus gave instructions to Peter, "Feed My sheep" (John 21:17 (NKJV)). The man who had once run in fear from a little servant girl, would later stand up before everyone in Jerusalem and preach the gospel. This was no small thing since the religious leaders still wanted to kill Peter. But many came to a saving belief in Jesus after this Spirit-led sermon.

The transformation in Peter was colossal, and Peter took his quiet faith in Jesus to his own crucifixion. The sifting Peter had faced was beyond hard. But what came out of it was a man on fire for Jesus—and only Jesus. At that point, nothing else, not even death, mattered.

I stood before the police chief. In my defense, I shared my faith and why I had made the decisions I had made in Jesus' name. No longer a man worried the gospel would ruffle feathers, I wasn't afraid of what he might think or what might happen to me. I knew Jesus was in my court and whatever happened to me was His will for my life. And I was okay with that.

I knew if the worst of the worst happened, there was a better plan awaiting me, somewhere around the corner. It didn't matter. The Shepherd was leading me, and I was simply following His voice. In the end, it was decided the punishment I faced would be cut in half. And now, the punishment is nothing but a memory in my mind.

Yet, the sifting remains. That difficult season was a turning point in my faith. And although sifting continues in my life, the Lord promised (through Paul) that He who had begun a good work in my life will complete it until the day of Jesus Christ (Philippians 1:6).

As I write this, I am being sifted once again—this time by injury and uncertainty. But the lessons I learned through that sifting have carried me on His eagle's wings. What is coming? I don't know. But He knows. And listening to His voice beckon to me in the darkness is enough because He is faithful. I am truly blessed.

One last thing . . .

A few years later, I looked into how the young lady's case had turned out. After I was thrown into internal affairs, the department chose to drop the shoplifting charge and put out an arrest warrant for the drug possession charge I told her I wouldn't hold against her. She was arrested and held over for a court trial. But the court dropped all the charges a few months later, after her drug-dealing boyfriend was murdered in front of her during what I can only believe was a bad drug deal.

If you think about it, this young lady, who had committed a crime, was cleared of all wrongdoing. And I was the one who was punished. Although I am not, by any means, comparing myself to Jesus, who took the punishment for all the sins of the world, trading His perfection for our sinfulness, this helped me to understand on the smallest level, what Jesus did for me. This is the gospel of Jesus Christ. And it is amazing.

Thank you, Jesus. You took the penalty of my sins upon Yourself, and You set me free. You saved me . . . you saved us all!

GOD'S GRACE MOVES YOU INTO A
NEW CHAPTER

I LOVE A GOOD MYSTERY. I suppose that's why I have enjoyed police work so much. It's like a journey through a story and the evidence that leads you to a final understanding of what happened. A really good "Who Done It" story has the ability to take us through a whole host of emotions. And if the author is really good, you'll never see the end coming.

No doubt, if you are like me, you are learning that God's will for your life is a mystery. As I walk along in the story He has laid out for me, I am learning that He is a really good storyteller.

After twelve years of committed patrol work, my perception of the job started to change. More accurately, my perception of what my mission was began to change. When I came in, I had my career planned out. But then, after finding the Lord, a "revealing" started to take place.

Coming into this profession, I had fully developed all my goals and dreams for my career. It was going to be awesome. The goals were a powerful motivator, and I followed the wise advice of those who had come before me. I tried to build relationships and a reputation that would get key people working on the assignments I wanted to be in—places like the SWAT team—to notice me.

Although I was told many positive things, I never realized even one of my initial career goals or dreams. Not even one. But it would prove to be for God's pleasure and glory as He began revealing the true mystery of my life, one I'm still uncovering.

The word used in the Bible for *mystery* is the Greek word *musterion*. This interesting word was used by Jesus and the Apostle Paul throughout the New Testament. It denotes a "secret that has yet to be revealed" or a "hidden thing, not obvious to the understanding."[1]

But we must get something cleared up. A *mystery* is not the same as *uncertainty*. A mystery has a truth to it, just not one that's known right away. And this makes sense. If you are reading a mystery story or trying to solve a crime, the truth is there—it just hasn't been revealed to you yet.

Your goal is to bring the mystery into the light. If you are successful, the truth is found, and it ceases to be a mystery. You might be uncertain of the truth when you start out. But it doesn't change the truth of the mystery, just the steps you must take to uncover that truth.

At the thought of failing, my career was now embattled with uncertainty. Did I make the right decision? Am I cut out for this? Am I wasting my time? It was easy to feel uncomfortable about my future in law enforcement as each year went by and I was continually being turned down for the work I so desperately wanted to do.

But the uncertainty I had been feeling started to change when I found Jesus. And little did I know that what looked like uncertainty for me, was actually a mystery being revealed, step by step, by the greatest Storyteller of all time.

After I was blessed to have a "Damascus Road" experience like Paul did in Acts 9, the Lord started to reveal the truth. It was the truth that the golden luster of all those dreams I had set out to accomplish was dim and tarnished in comparison to the story He was revealing about me. The mystery of my police career was starting to be revealed.

So, for six years, I had been working for the Lord in a city and in a time that had shown itself to be far darker than I ever expected it to be. But now I was starting to see that maybe police work was not the end, but rather a means to something greater. I promise you, when God is for you, when He is with you, and when you learn He has already written your story, then what's the worst that can happen?

All of this "street ministry" was going well. I was praying with and for those Jesus said were "the least of these" (Matthew 25:34–46). I was the tip of a spear the Lord was using to get the gospel into lives that would otherwise have never darkened the doorway of a church. And I was learning to love people in a deeper way.

Now, addicts and alcoholics were my target for love and grace, instead of the ridicule and harshness I had spent the first twelve years cultivating in my heart. I was truly a missionary in my own community, and I was seeing God's glory shining everywhere.

It was "faith-altering." It was amazing. I had found the "special assignment" I had been longing for, and I really felt like I had it figured out after a decade of trying.

Yet, when everything is comfortable and going well, expect that the Lord might tweak the story to reveal more of the mystery. This happened to me when I was injured on the job. After being on light duty for a few months, I wasn't sure where my career was actually going.

It was more of a mystery than it was at the beginning. There is truly no substitute for laying hands on someone who's having a horrible day, praying for them, and giving them a hug when they need it most. But there is not much lifeblood in the office, telephone, and computer. And it had been hard. It had been getting harder to remember that, in the eyes of my Savior, this was a well-devised "mystery" and not a heart-crushing "uncertainty."

In the Gospels, the Apostle Matthew records for us a similar story. There were good things happening; the directions seemed solid; the work was fruitful. But then a storm came. And uncertainty came. Then, more questions than answers came.

The Bible once again was pouring light into my personal life. And with light comes understanding. A continuous revealing of His great mystery.

After the Apostles had fed 5,000 men near the Sea of Galilee (about 10,000 if you include the women and children who were there), no doubt they were tired. But what they had just witnessed must have been the greatest miracle they had seen up to that point in Jesus' ministry. The Lord had taken five loaves of bread and two fish and multiplied them to feed the masses.

All four Gospels bring distinct details of an amazing story of servitude. No doubt, the Apostles must have felt like they were where God had called them to be. But after their spiritual high, Jesus did something the Apostles didn't expect. The Bible unfolds the story:

> Immediately Jesus made His disciples get into the boat and go before Him to the other side, while He sent the multitudes away. And when He had sent the multitudes away, He went up on the mountain by Himself to pray. Now when evening came, He was alone there. But the boat was now in the middle of the sea, tossed by the waves, for the wind was contrary. (Matthew 14:22–24 (NKJV))

A storm had come out of nowhere. And when the water started to flood into the boat and they couldn't control the situation, Jesus wasn't there to help them. These guys went from a sweet time of ministry, led by their Lord, to the fear-driven reality that they might be in big trouble.

To add to their fear, they didn't recognize Jesus when He finally got back to them. In the middle of the night, and in the pitch black, the Bible says they were afraid of the uncertainty:

> Now in the fourth watch of the night Jesus went to them, walking on the sea.
>
> And when the disciples saw Him walking on the sea, they were troubled, saying, "It is a ghost!" And they cried out for fear. (Matthew 14:25–26 (NKJV))

These men had spent every hour with Jesus for about two years. Why did they fail to recognize Him, even in the advancing storm?

How about you? Do you recognize Jesus when He's standing in the chaos of your storm? Do you see Him?

This is probably a good time for some advice. It would do our hearts well to recognize the Lord by looking back at His faithfulness in our troubled times. This will help us to believe the promise He has given about His faithfulness in the future.

Paul told young Pastor Timothy, "If we are faithless, He remains faithful" (2 Timothy 2:13 (NKJV)). And why does God remain faithful? Because faithfulness isn't just a behavior deemed important by the Lord—faithfulness *is* the Lord. And since He cannot change His nature, He cannot deny who He is!

When we read the Bible and understand exactly who God is (as He is plainly described throughout all the Scriptures), then we will recognize Him when He is standing there . . . no matter what's happening. But unfortunately, in our humanness—in our flesh—a lot of the time we don't recognize the revealing of God's mystery in the storm because we aren't well acquainted with His faithfulness. We only see the faithlessness of ourselves, which scares us in uncertain times.

The last call I took on the street—the call I was injured on— was a wrestling match with a teenager who was high on something fierce. I was unable to communicate with him because his mind was in another world. With my Biblical knowledge, I was pretty sure he was demonically influenced in one way or another. I say that because of the way he referred to himself in the third person, and he had a complete willingness and determination to destroy himself.

It's amazing. I know the demonic realm is real, and I truly believe that almost everything we face in life has a spiritual battle included in it. In fact, the Bible speaks to this important fact. It tells us:

> For we are not fighting against flesh-and-blood enemies, but against evil rulers and authorities of the unseen world, against mighty powers in this dark world, and against evil spirits in the heavenly places. (Ephesians 6:12 (NLT))

I know this verse well. But I'm not sure I was quite ready when I came face-to-face with a demon. And the amazing thing was: I found myself praying for the evil spirit to leave him (which was evident when I watched my body camera footage).

I didn't panic because I had studied God's Word and understood what I was up against. This kid's bizarre behavior wasn't uncertain, it was only a mystery I had uncovered while in my studies.

I also knew only God could help. Police training and years of experience couldn't help this kid. But the one true God could. So, I called on Him for help.

After we got him into the ambulance, I could still hear him screaming as the doors were closed and the bus drove away. I prayed with his family and friends. As you can imagine, they were spooked. And then I went and prayed at a church concerning what Jesus said about demons and demonic possession.

At the end of the shift, I spoke with the officer who had gone to the hospital with this young man. She told me that he continued screaming for a little while and then he just "woke up" and could speak and communicate plainly with her, just like Jesus did with the demoniac in Mark 5:1–20.

God is truly amazing. Miracles are happening all around you if you are watching.

But this was the last call I went on. I was doing work for the Lord, and my "street ministry" was going well. I was doing the types of things Jesus was teaching His disciples—I was being a light in a dark world. I was where I was supposed to be. I had found my niche.

But after the physical altercation, I started feeling pain. And the pain didn't go away in the following few days of rest. Then the little injury I tried to shake off turned out to be a bigger injury. And as the clouds began to build—and they got thicker and darker—the big injury could, in all actuality, be a career-ending one.

Where was God in all of this? Where was Jehovah Raffa, the "God-who-heals?" My little boat and my career were taking on water, and the winds were blowing. It was really dark, and I didn't know which way was up. And unlike the disciples, would I be able to recognize Jesus when He showed up?

So, I prayed, *Speak to me Jesus . . . I know your voice . . . Speak to me Jesus . . . I know your voice . . .*

If you continue reading the story, Jesus made Himself known to His beloved Apostles. They recognized their Savior, evidenced by the change from fear to boldness in Peter.

> But immediately Jesus spoke to them, saying, "Be of good cheer! It is I; do not be afraid."
>
> And Peter answered Him and said, "Lord, if it is You, command me to come to You on the water."
>
> So He [Jesus] said, "Come." (Matthew 14:27–29 (NKJV))

Oh, how amazing it would be to step out of a perfectly safe boat and onto the dangerous waves at the calling of Jesus, knowing safety and security are promised by the One who can protect you. Peter did just that as the story continued.

> And when Peter had come down out of the boat, *he walked on the water* to go to Jesus. But when he saw that the wind was boisterous, he was afraid; and beginning to sink he cried out, saying, "Lord, save me!"
>
> And immediately Jesus stretched out His hand and caught him, and said to him, "O you of little faith, why did you doubt?" And when they got into the boat, the wind ceased.
>
> Then those who were in the boat came and worshiped Him, saying, "Truly You are the Son of God." (Matthew 14:29–33 (NKJV); emphasis added)

Now, say what you want about Peter's *unbelief*. It seems a lot of people cast shade on him for "sinking." But think about it: Peter was the only person, other than Jesus, to walk on water.

And to make it a little more interesting—as prideful and outspoken as Peter was throughout the Gospels—he didn't personally say anything about that incident in the book authored by his nephew, Mark. Only the Apostle Matthew mentions Peter walking on water. Who knew?

But Jesus knew. He knew all along. To show Peter something about himself, Jesus was only waiting for the perfect time to reveal that part of Peter's mystery. And no doubt, Jesus knew about the coming storm, and He knew what He was going to do in that teaching moment.

How can you doubt a God who is that intuitive to your needs and development? Wow! As the Gospels and the Book of Acts continue, and in the two letters authored by Peter himself, we see very clearly how those steps of faith, along with the loving forgiveness of Jesus when Peter slipped up, made him the logical choice to build the Christian Church after Jesus had ascended into heaven.

And realize, this is God's truth for our lives too. It's not only for the Biblical elites. It's true for us as well.

I bring up this story because, while I was standing under the stars, talking to God, the Holy Spirit reminded me of the time Peter stepped out of the boat. And this led me to an interesting dilemma in my heart:

- Do I pray for the Lord to climb into *my* boat and make things better? Do I ask Jesus to heal me so I can go back to doing what I think He wants me to do (which truthfully, may be more about what I want to do)?

- Or do I say to Jesus the same thing Peter did? "Lord, if it is You, command me *to come to You* on the water" (Matthew 14:28 (NKJV); emphasis added).

Being in the boat is safe for me. It's all I've known for the last two decades. Peter, a career fisherman, was well acquainted with his boat. But he left what he knew to step out into something he didn't know.

From his own experience, Peter knew his boat was safe. But instead, Peter believed Jesus. And he did something new: he stepped out—literally—in faith. And Jesus was there to meet

Him where he was. For Peter, he stepped into uncertainty. But Jesus knew it was only a mystery that would quickly be revealed in Peter's heart.

So, how do you get this kind of faith in the Lord's plans for your life? Well, you must know, first off, that Jesus won't force you into His will. And He won't force you into His blessings either. This much I know to be true.

I have seen both sides of that coin. I have answered the call, and God has blessed me. I have also denied the call and have been left out of the blessing.

In all of this, I have learned Jesus will first beckon you to do something easy, maybe to get your faith "warmed up." It's because obedient steps will allow you to be "in step" with Him. Once you do that, you will be walking with Him and not contrary to Him—and then He can bless you immensely.

It reminds me of the story about a man, his withered hand, and a little bit of faith to do the uncomfortable thing Jesus asked him to do:

> And He [Jesus] said to the man who had the withered hand, "Step forward." Then He said to them [the religious rulers], "Is it lawful on the Sabbath to do good or to do evil, to save life or to kill?" But they kept silent. And when He had looked around at them with anger, being grieved by the hardness of their hearts, He said to the man, "Stretch out your hand." And he stretched it out, and his hand was restored as whole as the other. (Mark 3:3–5 (NKJV))

Don't miss something important here: the man with the withered hand was in the synagogue, on the most important day of the week, in front of a whole lot of really powerful men who were trying to find a reason to destroy Jesus. When Jesus told the man to step forward, the man was now on stage. He had a choice to make. Obey or don't obey. That is really all there is.

I wonder how long he thought about it. But the man took the small step of obedience. I have to believe this was not a comfortable place for him to be, but he had taken the first step.

Then, Jesus told him to reach out his hand. This was an even bigger step of faith because, if Jesus couldn't heal him, he would look foolish in front of all those men. What Jesus had asked of this guy must have sounded preposterous in his thoughts. His withered hand had been unusable for a long time. And certainly, it couldn't be healed.

Again, I wonder how long he thought about this one. But the man had faith to listen and to act. And he was rewarded; he was healed! The glory of God was displayed through this man's hand, not because Jesus did some magic, but because He controls creation.

Look, Jesus will bless you. And He will even do all the work it takes to get there. All you need to do is take the first step—one in faith.

Does this mean He will give you all your heart desires? No, because we are selfish.

Does it mean He will heal you of all your pains and sicknesses? No again—not in this life anyway—because He might use your sickness, pain, or heartache to move you somewhere your stubborn heart may not be willing to go on your own, due to your current comfort level.

Boy . . . that last one sounds familiar.

Over the last two months, God has further revealed to me part of the mystery in my life. As it turns out, I wasn't made to be a police officer. This is contrary to my heart because I can't count how many times I have thought to myself, "I was made for this job."

But lately, this has become a foolish idea. Sitting in front of a computer and answering phones has humbled me. No longer could I tout the pride I've always felt as I work the tough streets and the job I have come to love. No longer could I really lean on the personal identity I had built for myself as a "crime fighter." And no wonder, it's because I wasn't made to be a cop.

I now believe God has placed me here to let go of the false identity I had spent so long building up in my own head. Instead, I have a new understanding of what my identity truly is—that first and foremost, God created me to be His servant.

And being a police officer was what God allowed me to do to train me—to mold me and refine me into a better servant for His purposes. God knows me so well He knew I needed to become stronger, tougher, and more compassionate, and to realize through difficult situations and interactions with others, His true heart. And God's heart says, "Everyone matters because I love everyone and made them in My image."

But even this has its plateau, so to speak. And when that level is reached, God will move us on to something else . . . something more pressing . . . something higher . . . something closer to Himself.

I've found the following verse to be a more and more trustworthy saying in my life:

> [B]eing confident of this very thing, that He who has begun a good work in you will complete it until the day of Jesus Christ. (Philippians 1:6 (NKJV))

This means the Potter won't stop working until the vessel is made exactly like He wants it to be. When we understand the endgame is "the day of Jesus Christ," then whatever is short of that glorious day is just another rest stop on the trip to His glory in our lives. When we look at our lives in this way, we tend to loosen our grip on the things we think are important.

For me, I had been holding tightly to the idea that, without the patrol work, I would lose out on my street ministry. Yet, I found myself ministering and praying with someone who had called on the phone. I had the pleasure of doing this a number of times during this stormy season in my life.

This has allowed me to "bloom where I'm planted" and has revealed a special meaning to a Bible verse:

> For we are His workmanship, created in Christ Jesus for good works, which God prepared beforehand that we should walk in them. (Ephesians 2:10 (NKJV))

I didn't realize it before, but God revealed to me that the good works He is training me to complete are already out there, lined up for me in my future. If I'm walking in *His* ways, I will walk in those good works no matter where they are.

The uncertainty I had about doing God's work in a different career path was met with God's revealing of those good works in the mystery for my life. And since God is all-knowing and He knows my end, the works I so badly want to do are waiting for me—no matter where I go.

So, would God heal me back to the street ministry? Or would God move me out of the boat and onto the waves to meet Him where He is? I guess it's still a mystery.

And what does this all mean for me? Only the Lord knows. But I am excited to see how this mystery will reveal itself . . .

Lord, if it is You, command me to come to You on the water.

As I sit here recounting the stories included in this book, I have to admit: I never saw any of this coming when I started my career in law enforcement. I look back and chuckle to myself. God has a way of creating in us a life that has more twists and turns than a Hollywood movie. But if you're looking for a life that is orderly and predictable—you might be looking in the wrong place.

It has done my heart good to share these personal examples of God's grace. Yet, my desire wasn't to show you how God works in *my* life. I don't want you to feel as though my relationship with Jesus is out of your reach.

This book isn't about me at all. It isn't about my life or how much good I did. Instead, I simply wanted you to see that the God who led me all these years, is the same God who leads you.

My hope is, as you read these stories, you saw God in a new way. My desire is, when you open your eyes to the world around you, you'll see Him and believe.

The Bible tells us that He is closer than you can imagine (Acts 17:27), and His desire is to come into your home and dine with you. He is knocking . . . all you have to do is open the door (Revelation 3:20). Once you tune your heart into what *He* is doing in your life, you will see Him in everything around you, everywhere you go.

But what happens when life changes? Now that I'm retired from police work, I sometimes feel so far away from the "plan." I have spent the last year questioning God about this change in my life. How can I be a part of the miraculous works detailed in these stories while I'm tied to a desk, or even unemployed for a time?

The drastic life change didn't make all that much sense to me. But I learned quickly that God had a new plan. Just because my circumstances were different, it didn't mean He wasn't leading me through the same good works He has always been leading me through. The Bible tells us:

> For we are His workmanship, created in Christ Jesus for good works, which God prepared beforehand that we should walk in them. (Ephesians 2:10 (NKJV))

Over time, God has revealed to me that serving Him isn't tied to what a great job we have. It isn't tied to our education. Our identity isn't in these earthly ideas we seem to put all our stock into.

Instead, serving God is simply tied to our obedience and to His direction regardless of what we are doing at any given time. There are good works to be done no matter where we are. And God will provide the soil, the water, and the sunshine, so we can bear fruit wherever He has planted us.

This is important because God has many good works lined up for *you* to do for people wherever *you* are planted too. It might not be a thundering sermon or a massive financial blessing. It might simply be to show care to those our culture deems "untouchable." Or it might be to mentor a kid living on your street.

If you think you're exempt because you're not being paid by an official ministry to do the work . . . think again. We are *all* in the ministry if we belong to Jesus Christ.

And this opens you up to miraculous stories, just like the ones I have shared with you in this book. God is *always* working, and He wants you to be working with Him.

To that end, we must have the right mindset for the job. I think Peter sums this up beautifully when he writes:

> Finally, all of you should be of one mind. Sympathize with each other. Love each other as brothers and sisters. Be tenderhearted, and keep a humble attitude. Don't repay evil for evil. Don't retaliate with insults when people insult you. Instead, pay them back with a blessing. That is what God has called you to do, and He will bless you for it. (1 Peter 3:8–9 (NLT))

And God's grace? That unmerited and unearned favor from God that I have been talking about throughout this book? God will meet you with ample amounts of His wonderful grace wherever you love people in His name.

As you do, all kinds of avenues will open for you to see His miraculous love poured out before you. And we can come back together and rejoice in the good works the Lord has done in and through our lives (Acts 14:27). Just listen for His "still small voice" (1 Kings 19:12 (NKJV)), behind you, telling you which way to go (Isaiah 30:21).

Where does my life go from here? I'm not sure. But I know whatever the Lord has in His plans for me—it will be fantastic. I trust Him in that. All I can do is keep an open heart, have an obedient mind, and walk with Him one step at a time.

But honestly, at this point—that's not the most important question you should be asking. The real question is:

Where do *you* go from here?

NOTES

6. THE BRIDGE

1. Olive Tree Bible Software, ed., *Olive Tree Enhanced Strong's Dictionary* (n.p.: Olive Tree, 2011), Strong's number g4151.

8. FORGIVENESS—THE DUI (PART 1)

1. Marshall Shelley, *Ministering to Problem People in Your Church* (Bloomington, MN: Bethany House Publishing, 2013), 172.

9. RESTORATION—THE DUI (PART 2)

1. *Merriam-Webster*, s.v "providence (n.)," accessed May 29, 2023, https://www.merriam-webster.com/dictionary/providence.

10. A BRAZEN ATTACK

1. Maya Angelou Quotable Quote, Goodreads, accessed May 29, 2023, https://www.goodreads.com/quotes/846525-this-is-a-wonderful-day-i-have-never-seen-this.

11. THE WANDERING GRANDMA

1. "Those Who Leave Everything in God's Hand Will Eventually See God's Hand in Everything," *Chosen 509* (blog), January 26, 2018, https://chosen509.wordpress.com/2018/01/26/those-who-leave-everything-in-gods-hand-will-eventually-see-gods-hand-in-everything-unknown/.

14. TREASURE IN THE FIELD

1. "What Is Divine Providence?," Got Questions Ministries, accessed May 29, 2023, https://www.gotquestions.org/divine-providence.html.

16. A TOUGH DAY

1. *Dictionary.com*, s.v. "trust (n.)," accessed May 29, 2023, https://www.dictionary.com/browse/trust.

17. THE BASKETBALL

1. *Merriam-Webster*, s.v. "neighbor (*n.*)," accessed May 21, 2023, https://www.merriam-webster.com/dictionary/neighbor.
2. James Strong, *The New Strong's Expanded Dictionary of Bible Words* (Nashville: Thomas Nelson Publishing, 2001), 1319 ("plesion (*n.*)," g4139).

18. THE LETTER

1. *Merriam-Webster*, s.v. "sow (*v.*)," accessed May 21, 2023, https://www.merriam-webster.com/dictionary/sow.
2. Ibid., s.v. "scatter (*v.*)," accessed May 21, 2023, https://www.merriam-webster.com/dictionary/scatter.

20. A MYSTERY

1. Strong, *The New Strong's Expanded Dictionary of Bible Words*, 1246–47 ("musterion (*n.*)," g3466).

ABOUT THE AUTHOR

 Matthew Springer worked as a police officer in Colorado for twelve years before accepting Jesus Christ as his Lord and Savior. That prompted him to begin serving first responders and military personnel by overseeing a ministry called WAYpointONE. Six years later, an injury forced him to retire from police work.

Since retiring from the police force, Matthew continues to counsel and care for former and current first responders and military personnel. His heart is to help them through the trials and tribulations that come with the type of work they do.

Matthew lives in Colorado with his wife and children. You can find his Bible teaching on YouTube.

Website: WayPointOneMinistry.org
YouTube: @waypointoneministry4429
Facebook: Facebook.com/WayPointOneMinistry
Email: WayPointOneMinistry@gmail.com

Made in the USA
Monee, IL
16 October 2023

44666145R00141